Contract Law in Hong Kong

An Introductory Guide

Second Edition

Contract Law in Hong Kong

An Introductory Guide

Second Edition

Stephen D. Mau

HKU PRESS
香港大學出版社

Hong Kong University Press
The University of Hong Kong
Pok Fu Lam Road
Hong Kong
https://hkupress.hku.hk

ISBN 978-988-8208-43-2 (*Hardback*)
ISBN 978-988-8208-63-0 (*Paperback*)

British Library Cataloguing-in-Publication Data
A catalogue record for this book is available from the British Library.

Digitally printed

Contents

Preface to the Second Edition

Due to continuing popular demand, each book in this series of titles has been published again as a second edition while keeping the intention of the original book: to provide an introductory overview of the field of contract law to the general public.

As with the previous edition, the intention for this new edition is to have the main text provide a simplified and easy-to-understand introduction to contract legal principles. For those who are interested, more detailed explanations are found in the notes section, along with references to sources where more substantive information may be found. Also in the notes section are citations to relevant court cases and, where warranted, a discussion of the applicable cases.

This new edition has been updated to reflect the current state of the law in the territory and to include newer cases, both local and overseas. The organisation of this title has been revised for easier comprehension while keeping to the sequence in which a legally binding agreement is usually encountered: creation of the contract, interpreting the terms of the agreement, determining the related issue of whether there are any defects in the agreement, carrying out the terms of the contract, and the possible results if the agreement is not fulfilled. Additionally, further efforts have been made to use simple English in this edition.

It is hoped that these changes will make this edition even easier to use and to understand.

Preface to the First Edition

The purpose of this book is to provide general coverage of matters in the field of contract law. As such, this title is intended for the general public rather than legal professionals or those studying to become legal professionals. Consequently, this title is also suitable for beginners or students who require some legal knowledge but not to the extent of a legal practitioner. Other titles are available offering more extensive and more in-depth coverage of the subject for those who wish to pursue further studies.

The study of law is difficult—due to concepts, application, and/or technical terms—with language being an obstacle to many. With this and the readership in mind, we have attempted to strive for 'simple English' rather than more academic prose or technical legal language. Where technical terms are used, we have attempted to define those terms in simple English rather than using 'legalese'. Furthermore, we have provided a Chinese translation (in traditional characters) of most legal terms, either in the main text or in the endnotes.

This book contains endnotes for each of the chapters. In these endnotes, the reader may find additional information. This information may consist of more detailed explanations and/or discussions of the corresponding topic in the main text. This information may also consist of references to other sources where additional information on the particular topic may be found.

The author wishes to acknowledge the invaluable assistance provided by following individuals in the preparation of this publication: Sebastian Yat Fung Ko (高一鋒) BSc LLB (Hons), PCLL; Lam Terence (林蓬源); Krystal Lee Yeuk-ying (李若瑩); Li Tai Chiu, Ryan (李泰釗); Hazel Mah Hau-sung (馬孝笙); Pun Cheuk Lun, Eric (潘卓倫); and Shao Wai Chun, Wilson (邵尉晉).

Acknowledgements

I would like to take this opportunity to express my appreciation to the following individuals who assisted in the preparation of the second edition and who, as part of their job description, will accept total blame for any and all errors: Fong Man Hin (方文軒), Lam Tak Hing (林德興), Lit Ka Ki, Andy (列家麒), and Alix Povey.

Table of Cases

Table of Legislation

1
Introduction

A. Overview

This book is about the general legal principles concerning contracts. Rather than being a specialised textbook for law students, this book aims to introduce contract law to readers from different fields such as construction, accountancy, social work, and other individuals unfamiliar with this area of Hong Kong law. Some examples of topics which will be presented in this book include:

- What is a contract?
- How is a contract made?
- What are the different types of contract?
- When can a party to a contract 'legally escape' from its obligations under that contract?
- What happens when a party cannot 'legally escape' from its obligations under that contract?

Contracts have an important role in our life. Nearly every day, we make contracts with other people and organisations. It is obvious that a contract is formed when the buyer and the seller both sign an agreement, e.g., the sale of a flat. A contract is also formed when we have a meal in a restaurant or buy merchandise from a shop. Since contracts are such an essential part of daily life, it would be useful to have some knowledge of contract law. People could thus become more aware of possible legal issues and reduce the potential for disputes. This book is written with the purpose of increasing the awareness of these legal principles.

This publication will not cover all kinds of contracts. This book will cover contracts that are, in general, governed by the common law. Outside the scope of this work are the highly specialised contracts or contracts specifically regulated by law. Such types of contract are mainly governed by legislation instead of the common law contract principles on which this book focuses. For example, issues related to contracts of employment are categorised as *employment law*.[1]

However, before continuing on this subject of contract law, we should discuss a related matter. That matter is the common law legal system. Hong Kong, the United Kingdom, along with most of the Commonwealth, and the United States all follow the common law system. Continental Europe and China are examples of countries which follow the civil law legal system. The major difference between the two legal systems is that the common law legal system relies upon precedent.[2] *Common law* simply refers to the law common to everyone. *Precedent* refers to prior examples found in previous court decisions which would be followed in subsequent cases concerning the similar facts and issues. Consequently, this is the reason for referring to cases and for discussing cases in this book.

B. Organisation

This book is divided into seven chapters. We start first with the definition of *contract* which is provided later in this chapter. This is then followed by chapters about the different kinds of contract (i.e., what types or categories of contracts are there), elements of a contract (i.e., what is required to have a contract), and interpretation of a contract. The last three chapters respectively review the different ways to end a contractual relationship (i.e., a contract may end by a vitiating factor being present, completion of what is agreed by the parties in the contract, or one party failing to fulfil its obligations under the agreement so that the other party may sue in court). This book is arranged in a logical sequence of studying how a contract is formed, how its obligations are to be performed, and then how a contract ends.

C. Definition

What is a contract? How does a person know whether the agreement is simply an agreement or is a contract? Simply put, a contract is a legal agreement. A legal agreement refers to:

- an agreement;
- an agreement between at least two parties (a *party* can be, e.g., a person, a government, or a company); and
- one that the parties intend to be enforceable in court.

However, contracts and contract law are not always that simple and easy to understand. For example, there was an argument whether a contract should be defined as an agreement where 'there was an exchange of a promise for another promise', or as an agreement where 'obligations which are enforced or recognised by law'.[3] To complicate matters, there are general rules and exceptions to those general rules. For instance, the definition that a 'contract is an agreement giving rise to obligations which are enforced or recognised by law' is not always applicable.[4] For example, in a unilateral contract, '[person] A promises to do something if [person] B does something else'.[5] This means that when person B 'does something else', it is enough for person A to be bound to the contract. Person A and person B could be strangers and there would obviously be no agreement but a contract would still be formed. In another example, known as a *deed*, if a favour is made to a person, the promises contained in the deed are enforceable by him regardless of whether he is aware of them.[6] It can be seen that a legal contract can be formed without agreement. Conversely, even if there is agreement between two parties, the law does not always enforce the agreement. For example, if the parties are family members or if there are vitiating factors, the contract might not be enforceable.[7]

Nonetheless, in order to determine whether there is an agreement which a court would enforce, there has to be rules or legal principles which will guide the parties or a court in deciding whether there was:

- a legally enforceable agreement;
- what was meant by the agreement;
- how the agreement is to be carried out or enforced;
- what happens when one party fails to perform its obligations (known as a *breach* of contract) under the legally binding agreement; and/or
- how the other party (known as the *injured* party or the *innocent* party) should be compensated for a breach of the contract.

Therefore, we now review the meaning or definition of *contract*. More fully and formally described, a contract is a legally binding agreement between the parties to that agreement.[8] The term *contract* may refer to one or more of the following situations:

- a series of promises or acts that constitute a legally binding agreement
- the legal relationship that results from a series of promises or acts
- the document which represents that series of promises or acts or the performance of that series of promises or acts[9]

Contract law regulates the legality and thus the enforceability of that agreement.[10] The law of contract consists of case law which serves as precedent and which applies generally to all types of contracts. A party's liability under contract law depends on promises the parties have made to each other. Through their agreement, the parties make legally binding arrangements which will govern their relationship. Legal enforcement of a contract is done through the courts.

The basis of contract law can also be seen as reliance: to rely on receiving some future benefits as part of an agreed exchange and to reduce uncertainties related to that exchange. One purpose of a contract is to create a structure under which the parties organise their commercial relationship with certainty.[11] As such, an agreement may provide which party will be responsible for any loss of the goods in the transaction.[12] In other words, a contract can also be seen as an allocation of risk between the parties, e.g., the parties may agree that a seller in Hong Kong will accept the risk of damage to a shipment of goods until the goods are delivered to the buyer's warehouse in the United States.

2

Classifications of Contract

As mentioned above, a contract is a legally binding agreement. In this chapter, some of the types of legally binding agreements are presented although some of these agreements may fall into more than one category.[1]

A. Oral and Written Contracts

A legally binding agreement may have many different forms and may have many classifications.[2] Thus, a contract may be a completely oral agreement, a completely written agreement, or a partly oral and partly written agreement. As their classification implies, oral contracts are legally binding verbal agreements; written contracts are legally binding agreements in writing.

B. Contracts of Record and Simple Contracts

Another classification places legally binding agreements into three different categories: contracts of record, simple contracts, and contracts under seal (discussed in section F below).[3] *Contracts of record* are judgements and recognisances[4] placed in the record of a court. In law, this entry in the court's record implies an obligation rather than any agreement between the parties. Therefore, contracts of record are not contracts in the sense in which that term is generally used.[5]

Simple contracts are contracts without a seal and thus require consideration. Simple contracts are all contracts other than contracts of record or contracts under seal. Simple contracts may be expressed or implied, or partly expressed and partly implied. Expressed contracts state their terms in definite written or oral words. Implied contracts may be implied in law (where the terms are imposed by the law) or implied in fact (where the terms are inferred from the words or conduct of the parties).[6] Contracts that are partly expressed and partly implied have a combination of both characteristics.

C. Unilateral Contracts

There is another form of contracts: unilateral contracts. As discussed earlier, a *unilateral contract* is a contract where one party promises to do something in return for an act of a second party, as opposed to a promise. A unilateral contract is a:

> contract under which only one party undertakes an obligation. . . . It is to be noted, though, that the unilateral nature of the contract does not (in the ordinary case) mean that there is only one party, nor that there is no need for an acceptance or the provision of consideration by the other party. An example of a unilateral contract may be found in the case of an offer for a reward for the return of lost property: here, a contract is formed (at the latest) on the return of the property, this constituting the offeree's acceptance of the offer and the furnishing of consideration for the creation of the contract. Bilateral contracts comprise the exchange of a promise for a promise, e.g. if you promise to pay me £1,000, I promise to sell you my car.[7]

A unilateral contract, unlike a bilateral contract, thus involves a promise by one party and an act or action by another party.

In sum, where a person makes an offer of a reward for the return of a lost item, the offeror will be the only one bound by the offer. No one is obligated to search for the lost item. However, if, having learned of the offer, someone finds and returns the lost item, that individual is entitled to the reward.[8] In this type of contract, the offeror makes a promise while the offeree is expected to perform an act rather than to make a promise in return. One commonly cited example of a unilateral contract is the case of *Carlill v Carbolic Smoke Ball Co*, which will be discussed in Chapter 3, section B.ii.3.

D. Collateral Contracts

As mentioned previously, a collateral contract may arise during the negotiation of a main contract.[9] A *collateral contract* can be considered as a secondary agreement that stands alongside the main contract. In this subsidiary contract, a party is promised something as an inducement or incentive to enter into the main contract.[10] Thus, a collateral contract arises out of, or from, another legally binding agreement (the main contract) and is related to that contract.[11]

A collateral contract usually takes the form of a unilateral contract, under which one party offers that if the second party enters into the main contract, the first party will promise something else to the second party. The payment for the promise is the making of the main contract.[12] This may be seen in the case of *City & Westminster Properties v Mudd* [1958] 2 All ER 733. In this case, the tenant had been sleeping in the shop which he rented. During lease renewal negotiations, the landlord attempted to include a clause stating that the premises should not be used for lodging, dwelling or sleeping. The tenant objected, but was verbally informed that if he signed the lease, he could continue living in the basement. The landlord later tried to rely on the contract clause to put an end to the lease, claiming that the tenant breached the lease agreement by sleeping in the premises.[13] The court decided that the tenant proved that the oral promise made to him was part of a collateral contract. Because of the oral promise and relying upon this promise, the tenant had signed the main contract with the plaintiff.

E. Third Party Contracts and Privity

As will be discussed later in the section on *consideration*, it is possible for the benefit or the obligation of a contract be directed to a third party, that is, someone not a party to the contract. As will also be discussed in Chapter 7, a situation such as this might raise enforcement difficulties due to the principle of privity of contract. *Privity* refers to being a party to a contract. 'The common law doctrine of privity of contract means that a contract cannot (as a general rule) confer rights or impose obligations arising under it on any person except the parties to it.'[14] Thus, the general rule concerning privity is that no one can sue or be sued on a contract to which that person is not a party. In other words, the provisions of a contract are only applicable to the parties to that contract.

As privity of contract means that only a party to a contract can sue or be sued on that legally binding agreement, this principle will not allow a third party (i.e., a party not involved in the contractual relationship) to sue either party to the contract. A commonly used example to demonstrate this doctrine assumes that Alan owes a debt to Bob. Alan enters into a valid contract with Calvin to pay Bob. Calvin fails to pay Bob. Under the principle of privity of contract, Bob cannot sue Calvin. Rather, Bob would need to sue Alan who would then sue Calvin.[15]

Much has been written about the purpose and application of this principle along with the choices available to parties such as Bob. Conceptually, it has caused debate amongst the legal writers.[16] This theoretical debate has carried over to the courts which have created ways to evade this doctrine, such as the notion of an agent, a trust, and the application of certain land covenants.

Legislation has also been enacted in order to limit the application of the privity principle. For example, in the United Kingdom there is the Contracts (Rights of Third Parties) Act 1999, and in Hong Kong there is the Married Persons Status Ordinance (Cap 182). Additionally, in Hong Kong, the Law Reform Commission issued a Consultation Paper[17] in 2004 and a Report on Privity of Contract[18] in 2005 suggesting that the territory enact similar legislation to that adopted in the United Kingdom. This was done with the passing of the Contracts (Rights of Third Parties) Ordinance (Cap 623) at the end of 2014. This law came into effect at the beginning of January 2016.[19]

F. Formalities/Contracts Required to Be in Writing

We have discussed above the most common forms or types of contracts. Additionally, there are other types which, although not as common as the types of legally binding agreements above, should be mentioned. For these contracts, certain formalities need to be followed as to: form, content, a requirement to be in writing, or execution.

One type is a contract known as a *contract under seal*, also known as a *contract made by deed*[20] or as a *specialty contract*.[21] This type of legally binding agreement takes effect through its solemn form rather than through general contract principles. Therefore, a specialty contract must be signed, sealed, and delivered.[22] One reason for requiring this form is that a specialty contract requires no consideration and has the seal of the signer attached. A contract under seal must be in writing and is conclusive between the parties when signed, sealed, and delivered. Delivery is made either by actually handing it to the other party or by stating an intention that the deed be operative even though it is kept in the possession of the party that signed this document.[23] In Hong Kong, contracts under seal are found mainly in real estate transactions, government construction contracts, and certain insurance contracts. One purpose of a deed is explained below.[24]

> The basis of the common law of contract is bargain. A party who wants to enforce a contract must show that he or she has given

> consideration. If A says to B "On your twenty-first birthday, I will give you $100,000 to set you up in life" and B says "Thank you", there is certainly an agreement between them. But there is no contract . . . because B has not given anything in return for A's promise. Each party to a contract must give something . . . to the other in exchange for what he or she gets. It is not a contract if one party takes rights without incurring corresponding duties. But consideration is not necessary if the contract is by deed.
>
> . . . Moreover, it is possible to make a gift . . . which will be binding without consideration. It is the promise which is not binding without consideration, not the transfer of property. . . . if the subject matter is of such a nature that delivery is not possible, such as a promise, then a deed must be used.[25]

Another category pertains to contracts which must observe some kind of formality in order to be valid. This formality usually requires that the agreement be written or be written in a particular way. Thus, for the purposes of this section, we refer to these as *contracts required to be in writing*. These actually are contracts which are required by law either to be in writing or to be evidenced in writing, i.e., something in writing which proves the existence of the agreement. Some of the most common contracts required to be in writing are legally binding agreements that affect land, e.g., purchase and sale agreements, certain leases, easements, and mortgages.[26] Another example which requires both a particular formality and the writing requirement is a power of attorney, which is a document giving one person the right to act on another's behalf. The Powers of Attorney Ordinance (Cap 31) requires that, under certain circumstances, a written document be signed and sealed in the presence of two attesting witnesses.[27]

Other Hong Kong ordinances which require a legally binding agreement to be in writing or evidenced in writing include the following examples:

- Arbitration Ordinance (Cap 609)
- Bills of Exchange Ordinance (Cap 19)
- Money Lenders Ordinance (Cap 163)
- Marine Insurance Ordinance (Cap 329)
- Contracts for Employment Outside Hong Kong Ordinance (Cap 78)

3
Elements of a Contract

In this chapter, we discuss the requirements in order to have a valid contract. We will look at the difference between an *agreement* and a legally binding agreement. In other words, how and when does an agreement become a contract?

An agreement is legally enforceable (i.e., considered a *contract* by the law) if the agreement contains all of the following elements:

- All the parties have the intention to create a legal relationship.
- There must be consent or agreement between these parties.
- There must be consideration for the agreement or else the agreement must be made under seal.
- The terms of the agreement are certain.
- The parties to the agreement have the capacity to enter the agreement.[1]

The first three requirements will be presented immediately below. The last two requirements will be discussed later in Chapter 4 and Chapter 5 respectively.

A. Intent

To have a valid contract, the parties must have the intention to create a legally binding relationship. In other words, the parties must intend the agreement to be enforceable in court. This is a major difference from an agreement, such as a social agreement. In some agreements, such as between friends to have lunch together, the parties may not have the intention of suing in court if the other party does not show up for lunch. How is this intention to be legally bound determined to be present or absent in an agreement?

Intention is determined objectively from the circumstances, including the nature of the words used or the conduct of the party making the offer. In commercial transactions, there is an assumption that the agreement is intended to be legally binding. In social or domestic situations, unless the parties state otherwise, the law presumes that such agreements are not intended to be legally binding. In the case of *Balfour v Balfour* [1919] 2 KB 571, there was an agreement between spouses for the payment of a monthly allowance to the wife (who remained in England because of medical reasons while the husband worked overseas). The wife attempted to enforce this promise. The court determined this agreement to be legally unenforceable as it was a domestic agreement. The court presumed that the parties did not intend to create a legal relationship. In the case of *Jones v Padavatton* [1969] 1 WLR 328, the court decided that family agreements were dependent upon the parties' good faith to keep their promises and that the parties did not intend to make legally binding agreements.

B. Agreement

Once we have determined whether the parties to an agreement intend to be legally bound by that agreement, we need to examine whether the parties had come to any agreement. Note that some individuals would prefer to reverse the order of our review, that is, to determine firstly whether there was any agreement before deciding whether the agreement is legally binding. This can be done as this particular order is flexible. What is important is that all of the above elements of a contract are present before concluding that there is a legally binding agreement.

There must be a legally binding agreement between the parties before one party can enforce another party's promise.

> Agreement is usually reached by the process of offer and acceptance . . . the law requires that there be an offer on ascertainable terms which receives an unqualified acceptance from the person to whom it is made.[2]

To determine the existence of a contract and its provisions, courts have used this approach to determine the precise words and conduct which result in offer and acceptance. Some courts are willing to be flexible where the words and conduct are unclear. These courts would look at all the circumstances at the time when the agreement was made in order to determine whether a contract was formed. Recall, however, for certain particular agreements, such as contracts under seal, identification of offer and acceptance is not necessary.

We, too, will use this offer-and-acceptance approach. Contracts under seal are comparatively less frequently used, so we firstly will concentrate on offer-and-acceptance and discuss contracts under seal in a later section. We start with the topic of *offer* below.

i. Offer

An *offer* is a promise to do (or not to do) something in the future. An offer is also a display of willingness to enter into a contract on specified terms, made in such a way that a reasonable person would expect acceptance to result in a legally binding agreement.[3] Thus, once an acceptance of an offer is made, a contract exists between the parties.

The party making an offer is the *offeror* (also referred to as the *promisor*). The party to whom this offer is made is the *offeree* (also referred to as the *promisee*). An offer can be made expressly, i.e., by definite spoken or written words. An offer can also be made impliedly, i.e., by conduct or by law. An example of an implied contract by conduct is a bus ride to work. A bus pulls up to the bus stop. You get on the bus and pay the specified bus fare. By conduct, you and the bus company have entered into a legally binding agreement. No words need to be spoken or written in this example. An example of an implied contract by law would involve contract terms imposed by law rather than negotiated by the parties.

An offer must be made with the intention that upon acceptance, the offer becomes binding. Once the offer becomes binding, there is offer and acceptance, i.e., consent or agreement by the parties to a contract.

> When determining whether an offer had been made, one should identify 'an expression of willingness to contract on certain terms made with the intention that it shall become binding as soon as it is accepted by the person to whom it is addressed'. The person effecting such expression is the offeror even though he may not have initiated the contact.
>
> It is difficult at times to determine which statements or which acts constitute an offer. It is particularly difficult where the parties are indiscriminate with the use of words. The test of an offer is the intention of an expression and not the words used.[4]

Thus, a statement will not be an offer if it is merely intended to supply information. This is demonstrated in the case of *Harvey v Facey* [1893] AC 552. One of the main issues considered by the court involved the following question: Did a legally binding sale and purchase agreement exist for the sale of a property named *Bumper Hall Pen*? Harvey had telegraphed Facey, asking, 'Will you sell Bumper Hall Pen? Telegraph lowest price for Bumper Hall Pen.' Facey answered, 'Lowest price for Bumper Hall Pen [would be] £900.' Harvey responded by agreeing to buy the property for Facey's price of £900. All these telegrams were duly received by Harvey and Facey.

Harvey attempted to enforce the supposed contract by arguing that the exchange of telegrams showed an implied agreement by Facey to sell. Harvey argued that by answering the second question concerning price, Facey impliedly agreed to sell Bumper Hall Pen for £900.

The court, however, rejected this argument and observed that any contract must be determined from the telegrams. Facey's response was a statement of the lowest price at which he would sell. The telegrams contained no implied contract to sell to the person making the inquiry. The exchange of telegrams was part of the preliminary contractual negotiation before the parties could enter the contract.

The court determined that Facey's telegram was only binding on him as to the £900 sale price and that the telegram was merely an offer to sell the property at a price of £900. Harvey's reply telegram could only be treated as an acceptance of Facey's offer to sell the property at a price of £900. In other words, Harvey's telegram was an offer to purchase the property for £900 to be accepted by Facey. Thus, the contract could only be completed if Facey had accepted Harvey's last telegram.

In summary, the court found that there was no contract between these parties for the following reasons:

- The first telegram asked two questions. The first question concerned the willingness of Facey to sell the property to Harvey. The second question asked the lowest price. The word *telegraph* used by Harvey addressed only the second question.
- Facey replied to the second question only. By stating that £900 was his lowest price, Facey gave a precise answer to a precise question—the selling price.
- Harvey's next telegram wrongly treated Facey's statement of a £900 sale price as an unconditional offer to sell to Harvey at that stated price.

1. Bilateral and unilateral contracts

An offer can be made to a particular person, a particular group of persons or to the general public. Where the offer is made to a particular person or a particular group of persons, a contract is formed when the offeree accepts the offer. This type of contract is known as a *bilateral contract*. Bilateral contracts are generally formed after negotiations have taken place resulting in a promise in exchange for another party's promise. Both parties make binding promises and one promise is consideration for the other promise. The same principle applies in multilateral contracts.

Recall that acceptance of an offer requires the offeree to know of the offer. The offer must be communicated to an offeree and an acceptance must be communicated to the offeror. Only the offeree is entitled to accept, no one else is entitled to accept, even if that person has learnt of the offer. One author succinctly and simply summarised this type of contract:

> A bilateral contract consists of an exchange of promises. A 'bilateral' offer, therefore, seeks a *promise* in return, e.g., Offer—'I [promise that I] will sell you my car for £500.' Acceptance—'I [promise that I] will pay £500 for your car.'[5]

By contrast, in a *unilateral contract*, there is an offer by the offeror followed by performance by the offeree rather than a return promise by the offeree. Unilateral contracts may arise in advertisements of rewards, or agreements on contingency fees (e.g., estate broker's contract). If an offer is made to the public at large, the offer is accepted when a person performs the act requested in the offer. Then, a unilateral contract is formed.

Again, a unilateral contract cannot be created by an offeree's return promise to perform. With a unilateral contract, only one party makes a promise—the offeror. The offeree must complete the required performance in order for there to be acceptance.[6] The offeree does not make any promises. For example, the offeror communicates a promise to pay $1,000 to anyone who swims across Victoria Harbour. For the offeree to be paid the $1,000, the offeree must swim across Victoria Harbour. The offeree cannot simply promise to swim across the harbour. Compare this to a bilateral contract, where negotiations have taken place resulting in a promise in exchange for another's promise.[7]

Traditional theory concerning unilateral contracts was that the offeror may withdraw the offer at any time prior to complete performance, even if the offeree has started performance. Today, the commonly accepted view is that the offeror cannot withdraw the offer once the offeree has started to perform the required act.[8] Further, the offeree is not required to notify the offeror of performance unless the offeror is located far away and would be unaware of the performance. Notification prevents the offeror from entering a contract with another person for the same purpose.

2. *Termination of offer*

An offer terminates when there is a:

- rejection of the offer by the offeree;
- revocation of the offer by the offeror;
- lapse of time;
- death or other incapacity of one of the parties; or
- failure of the condition to materialise where the offer is conditional.

The two most common methods of ending an offer are by rejection or revocation. If an offer has been rejected by the offeree, the offer cannot be later accepted. The case of *Lee Siu Fong Mary v Ngai Yee Chai* [2006] 1 HKC 157 applied this principle. In this case, Lee made loans to Ngai which were only partially repaid. Ngai offered to repay the outstanding amount over six years. Lee rejected the offer. Seven years later, Lee sued in court to recover the outstanding amount. The court stated:

> 14. The truth of the matter is that having rejected this offer or proposal on 21 May 1995 there was no further offer or proposal from the defendant for the plaintiff to accept later on. There was no evidence that the defendant had intended to leave this offer open so that it may be accepted by the plaintiff at some later time.
>
> 15. An offer whether it is called by the name of proposal or suggestion is simply an expression of willingness to contract made with the intention that it is to become binding on the person making it as soon as it is accepted by the person to whom it is addressed . . . If the offer was rejected by the plaintiff, she could not unilaterally revive it by saying that she had later accepted it.
>
> 16. . . . the fundamental point is that there must be an offer or representation made by one party for the other party to accept or rely upon. The so-called representation by the defendant in this case was exactly the same offer he had made and rejected by the plaintiff. Once this was rejected then there was nothing for the plaintiff to rely upon.[9]

Another common method of terminating an offer is by the offeror withdrawing the offer at any time before it is accepted. This withdrawal is known as *revocation* of the offer or as *revoking* the offer. If the offeror revokes the offer, a notice of revocation must be communicated to the offeree before acceptance is made. Revocation is effective if it is communicated in a manner equal to or greater than the way the offer was publicised, even though the offeree has no knowledge of the revocation.

The general rule is that an acceptance of an offer must be communicated to the offeror before revocation of the offer or before expiration of the offer through the lapse of time. An exception is where there is an offer of reward.

3. Options

An option is where an offeror promises to keep the offer open for a stated period and the offeree pays for this promise. This is a separate contract, known as a *collateral contract*,[10] between the offeror and the offeree that the offer would be kept open for that stated period of time. The mere promise by an offeror to keep the offer open is not legally binding, as the offeror's promise requires consideration unless the promise is made by deed.

ii. Acceptance

The offeror, as part of the offer, may specify the method of acceptance by the offeree. *Acceptance*, then, is the unequivocal and unconditional agreement to all the terms made in the offer, including the method of acceptance. This acceptance must be made with the knowledge of the existence of the offer.[11] The offer is the reason for the acceptance and there must be a *meeting of the minds* prior to performance of the contract. For example, two identical offers, one to buy and one to sell, that *cross* in the mail do not create a contract if neither offer was accepted with the knowledge of its existence.

Acceptance of an offer by the offeree must be given voluntarily and freely. Acceptance may be communicated to the offeror orally, in writing, by conduct, or a combination of these. Again, if the offer required a certain method of acceptance, the offeree must make acceptance in that required manner. An offeror, however, cannot require silence as the method of acceptance. Where an acceptance is not identical to the offer (e.g., introducing new or different terms, or new or different conditions), the acceptance is not valid. In such cases, the *acceptance* may be interpreted either as a rejection of the offer or a counter-offer.

1. Postal Rule

An exception to the general rules concerning acceptance is the *Postal Rule*, also known as the Mailbox Rule.[12] Under this rule, the acceptance of an offer by post is considered to be made when the letter containing that acceptance is posted, i.e., placed in the control of the postal service.[13] This rule also applies to the use of telegrams.[14] Should the message never arrive, an agreement is nevertheless concluded, provided there is no fault on the part of the offeree. However, the offeree's acceptance posted after his initial rejection (i.e., the offeree had a change of mind) is not effective until it is received. The application of the Postal Rule can become complicated when the time of acceptance or revocation of an offer is in dispute, particularly where the letter is incorrectly addressed, delayed or lost.

The Postal Rule does not apply: where an offeror expressly or impliedly excludes this rules' application, or where an acceptance is made by instantaneous communication, e.g., e-mail, telephone, telex or facsimile. The reason for excluding instantaneous communication is that an acceptance of an offer made by such methods of communication is usually acknowledged by the recipient.[15] Further, the offeree would know whether the attempt to make acceptance was successful so that appropriate action can be taken. By comparison, a person who makes acceptance by post may never be aware of any loss or delay, and may not have the opportunity to correct the problem in time. Therefore, instantaneous communications are generally governed by the general rule that an acceptance must be actually communicated to and received by the offeror.[16]

> Fax messages seem to occupy an intermediate position between postal and instantaneous communications. The sender will know at once if his message has not been received at all, or if it has been received only in part, and in such situations the mere sending of the message should not amount to an effective acceptance. It is also possible for the entire message to have been received, but in such a form as to be wholly or partly illegible. Since the sender is unlikely to know, or to have means of knowing, this at once, it is suggested that an acceptance sent by fax might well be effective in such circumstances. The same reasoning should apply to messages sent by electronic means, *e.g.* by e-mail or in the course of website trading: here again the effects of unsuccessful attempts to communicate should depend on whether the sender of the message knows (or has the means of knowing) at once of any failure in communication.[17]

The case of *Susanto-Wing Sun Co Ltd v Yung Chi Hardware Machinery Co Ltd* [1989] 2 HKC 504, involved disputes over the use of faxes and the place where the contract was made. There were two contracts for the sale of goods and machinery by the defendant to the plaintiff. The defendant, Yung Chi, in Taiwan faxed each of the two agreements to the plaintiff in Hong Kong. Immediately upon receipt of each agreement, the plaintiff accepted the agreement by signing and faxing it back to the defendant.

The court stated:

> It appears however, that the contracts were concluded in Taiwan and not in Hong Kong; because it was in Taiwan that the communication of the plaintiff's acceptance of the offer was received by the defendant. The rule relating to communications by telex is now well settled and the same rule must . . . apply to communications by facsimile. The general rule is that as between . . . [the parties] the contract, if any, is made when and where the acceptance is received . . . the rule to which I have referred applies to instantaneous communication between principals.[18]

2. *Counter-offer*

What happens in a situation where there is an offer and the offeree accepts the offer except with slightly different terms? For example, what is the result if the offeror offers to sell a pen for $10 and the offeree accepts but at a price of $8? This act by the offeree is an example of a counter-offer. A counter-offer is not an acceptance of an offer. Rather, a *counter-offer* is usually considered to be a rejection of the original offer and the making of a new offer by the offeree. Withdrawal of the counter-offer does not restore the original offer so as to allow the offeree to accept the original offer.

An offeree's request for information, or even an enquiry to negotiate a better price, is not a counter-offer. As the court explained in *Stevenson, Jaques & Co v McLean* (1880) 5 QBD 346, the request for information is 'a mere inquiry which should have been answered and not treated as a rejection of the offer'.[19] In this case, the defendant offered to sell 3,000 tonnes of iron at forty shillings per ton. The offer remained valid until Monday. The plaintiff sent its first telegram early Monday requesting, 'Please wire whether you would accept forty [shillings per tonne] for delivery over two months, or if not what is the longest limit you would accept.'[20] Receiving no reply, the plaintiff later that day sent a second telegram indicating acceptance at forty shillings cash. In the interim, the defendant had sold the goods elsewhere without informing the plaintiff until after the plaintiff had sent the second telegram. The court decided that a contract existed between the plaintiff and the defendant.

3. *Invitation to treat*

There are situations where it is unclear whether one party is making an acceptance of an offer or is being asked to make an offer. An *invitation to treat* is a negotiating statement and a request for an offer.[21] 'An invitation to treat is a mere declaration of willingness to enter into negotiations; it is not an offer, and cannot be accepted so as to form a binding contract.'[22]

Under these circumstances, customers are invited to make an offer to buy at a particular price and traders keep the power to decide whether to accept the price offered. Thus, the traders do not have the required intent to give the other party the power to create a contract. Merely fixing a price does not imply an offer to buy or to sell. For example, the display of goods by a merchant, price lists, circulars, and advertisements for goods and services are normally considered to be invitations to treat.[23]

The distinction between offer and invitation to treat is found, respectively, in the intention or in the absence of an intention to be legally bound as soon as the addressee accepts the terms stated. An invitation to treat is a request to the other party to negotiate rather than an invitation to communicate an acceptance.[24] In the above example, an invitation to treat is an offer by the trader to the customer to make an offer.

At times it may be difficult to distinguish an invitation to treat from an offer. The distinction is whether the offeror shows an intention to be legally bound, and whether the language of the offer allows the offeree to reasonably understand that the power to accept the offer exists. One academic source explains:

> A communication by which a party is invited to make an offer is commonly called an invitation to treat. It is distinguishable from an offer primarily on the ground that it is not made with the intention that it is to become binding as soon as the person to whom it is addressed simply communicates his assent to its terms. A statement is clearly not an offer if it expressly provides that the person who makes it is *not* to be bound merely by the other party's notification of assent but only when he himself has signed the document in which the statement is contained.[25]
>
> . . . the distinction between offer and invitation to treat is often hard to draw, as it depends . . . on . . . the intention of the person making the statement in question.[26]

An example of the difficulty in making this distinction between an offer and an invitation to treat can be found in *Carlill v Carbolic Smoke Ball Co* [1893] 1 QB 256. In this case, a manufacturer published an advertisement during an influenza epidemic, claiming its smoke balls could cure certain illnesses. In addition, the manufacturer stated that anyone who bought one of its smoke balls, used it as directed, and then caught influenza, would be paid £100. Mrs. Carlill bought and used a smoke ball.

She nevertheless caught influenza and claimed £100 from the company. The company argued that the advertisement was not an offer which could create a contract by acceptance. The court, however, considered that since the advertisement stated the company had deposited £1,000 in its bank in order to show its sincerity, reasonable people could consider this as indicating the promise to pay £100 was serious, and that this act created a binding obligation.

Thus, whether an advertisement constitutes an offer depends upon its wording and its natural meaning. If an advertisement is very specific and clear, it may amount to an offer (e.g., a limited offer to the first 10 people entering the store). This may be accepted without qualification. An offer in this manner may be accepted by anyone unless there is some restricted class of persons to whom the advertisement is directed. Even then, any member of that class may accept.

However, one source notes:

> Some recent developments have had the effect of altering traditional rules, as for example as has occurred in the case of a tender. Generally, the tender process is treated as three distinct parts: the invitation to treat by the party inviting tenders, the offers from those interested and the acceptance by the invitor of one of those offers. Acceptance results in a binding contract on the terms set out in the invitation to treat. In several cases, various courts have re-categorised the invitation to treat as an offer. This means there are two possible contracts. The first is the traditional contract which arises under the tender. The second is a collateral contract under which the invitor acts as an offeror because he expressly or by implication agreed to consider all offers. Failure to do so gives rise to action for damages for loss of chance. As a corollary, the party submitting the tender may not be able to withdraw.[27]

Similarly, in auctions, the auctioneer invites bids. The potential buyer makes an offer by making a bid, which the auctioneer must accept when the auctioneer's hammer falls. The buyer may withdraw the offer at any time before the hammer falls. If the bid is withdrawn, it does not revive an earlier bid by the previous bidder. Thus, the bidding must restart. At an auction, the auctioneer's invitation for bids is impliedly made *with reserve* allowing the auctioneer to remove the item for auction if a sufficient price is not bid. If, however, an auction is expressly made *without reserve*, then the auctioneer cannot withdraw the item unless no bid was made at all.

C. Consideration

At its simplest, *consideration* is payment, usually in the form of money. However, the concept and types of consideration can be much more. The case of *Currie v Misa* (1875) LR 10 Ex 153 defined *consideration* as some right, interest, profit or benefit accruing to one party, or some forbearance, detriment, loss or responsibility given, incurred or undertaken by the opposite party.[28] The case of *Dunlop Pneumatic Tyre Co v Selfridge & Co* [1915] AC 847, also defined *consideration* as: 'an act or forbearance of one party, or the promise thereof, is the price for which the promise of the other is bought, and the promise thus given for value is enforceable'.[29] In other words, consideration is a bargained for action (or the promise not to take action) or a return promise to pay.[30] Consideration is that which is actually given or accepted in return for a promise, and that which has real value. Consideration can be analysed as being either a benefit to the offeror or a detriment to the offeree. Consideration may be something other than money (e.g., a promise).

> In other words, if one receives something to which he is not entitled he has received a benefit even though that thing may in fact not be beneficial to him. And, if one does something he is obligated to do or refrains from doing something he is entitled to do, he suffers a legal detriment even though the act or omission may in fact be beneficial to him.[31]

Note, however, that an illusory promise (a promise that is not actually binding upon the promisor) does not constitute valid consideration. For example, one party might reserve the right to alter or revoke the contract at any time.

It is unnecessary that the party making the promise should benefit by the consideration. It is sufficient if the party receiving the promise does some act from which a third party or person benefits.[32]

There is an exception to the requirement for consideration. This exception concerns a particular type of contract known as a *deed* or *contract under seal*. In situations involving this type of contract, a seal replaces the need for consideration. This subject has been discussed in Chapter 2, section F and will be reviewed in more detail at the end of this chapter.

i. Adequacy and Sufficiency of Consideration

Consideration need not be adequate although it must be sufficient at law.[33] Therefore, $100 can be sufficient consideration in law for the possession of a house, even though the house is worth much more in monetary value.[34]

> Under the doctrine of consideration, a promise has no contractual force unless *some* value has been given for it. But as a general rule the courts do not concern themselves with the question whether "adequate" value has been given, or whether the agreement is harsh or one-sided. The fact that a person pays "too much" or "too little" for a thing may be evidence of fraud or mistake . . . [b]ut it does not of itself affect the validity of the contract . . .
>
> The general common law rule discussed above is subject to a number of exceptions . . . the general rule applies that the courts will enforce a promise so long as *some* value for it has been given.[35]

Love and affection is not considered valid consideration. The rationale is that although:

> consideration need not be adequate, it must be "of some value in the eye of the law," that is, it must be capable of estimation in terms of economic or monetary value, even though there may be no very precise way of quantifying that value. This is one reason why there is no consideration for a promise made "in consideration of natural love and affection," and why in *Thomas v Thomas* the testator's desire that his widow should live in his house was not part of the consideration for the executors' promise to allow her to do so.[36]

Consideration must also move from the offeree. Unless the offeree has provided consideration for the offeror's promise, the offeree cannot enforce the contract. As previously mentioned, consideration needs not go to the offeror. Consideration may move to wherever the agreement stipulates, such as to a third party:

> While consideration must move from the promisee [i.e., offeree], it need not move to the promisor [i.e., offeror]. It follows that the requirement of consideration may be satisfied where the promisee suffers some detriment at the promisor's request, but confers no corresponding benefit on the promisor. Thus the promisee may provide consideration by giving up a job or the tenancy of a flat, even though no direct benefit results to the promisor from these acts. It also follows that the promisee may provide consideration by conferring a benefit on a third party at the promisor's request: e.g. by entering into a contract with the third party . . .

> [T]he rule that consideration need not move to the promisor equally applies where the consideration consists simply in a benefit conferred by the promisee without loss to himself. Here the requirement of consideration is satisfied if a benefit is conferred either on the promisor or on a third person at his request.[37]

ii. Past Consideration

Consideration must be more than the performance of an existing duty. A party required by an existing contract to perform certain obligations does not provide any consideration for another contract by promising to fulfil those pre-existing obligations. Since one party is already legally entitled to the promises contained in the contract, to receive those promises again is of no additional legal benefit. Similarly, since one party is already legally obligated to provide those promised items or services, to do so is no additional legal detriment. Such existing contractual obligations provide no additional burden for a new contract. However, fulfilling an existing contractual obligation between the two parties for the benefit of a third party is new consideration. Here, the promisor gives the third party the right to sue in the event of non-performance by the promisor. This is a right the third party did not have until the promise was made.

> While consideration may be executory or executed, it must not be "past". Past consideration exists when the apparent act, or promise, of consideration occurred *before* the promisor's promise. A simple illustration would be provided by the case of a drowning man, D, who cries for help. X generously rescues D who promises X a reward in gratitude. Since X's act of rescue occurred *before* D's promise, it is past consideration and the rule is that "past consideration is no consideration". The concept of past consideration is easy to understand if one bears in mind the requirement that consideration must be the "price" of the other party's promise: the act of rescue may well be a detriment to the rescuer but it cannot be the price of the rescued person's promise since that promise has not yet been made.[38]

Consequently, a promise supported only by past consideration is generally unenforceable because the benefit given or detriment incurred is not the result of the present promise. If one party has fully performed before obtaining a promise from the other party, there is no bargain or consideration for that promise. However, there are exceptions to this rule. We now discuss some of these exceptions below.

For example, as previously discussed, one exception is the fulfilment of an existing contractual obligation to a third party. Assume that there is a contractual relationship between Alan and Bob. Calvin (the third party) enters into a contract with Alan to pay him in order to ensure that Alan performs his contract with Bob. There is consideration in this scenario because Alan gives Calvin, the third party, a right to sue in the event of non-performance.

Another exception is in situations where:

- the act (or promise) must have been done at the promisor's request;
- the parties must have understood that the act required payment (cash or some other benefit); and
- the payment must have been legally enforceable had it been promised in advance.[39]

A final exception to the general rule that consideration cannot be past may arise from statute. For example, section 27 of the Bills of Exchange Ordinance (Cap 19) provides that valuable consideration may consist of an antecedent debt or liability. In other words, a debt or obligation that precedes the making of a bill can be good consideration under this law. A cheque is an example of a bill of exchange.

iii. Performing an Outstanding Obligation

Performing or promising to perform an obligation already owed to the same party under a prior contract cannot be consideration for a new promise. In the case of *Stilk v Myrick* (1809) 2 Camp 317, a ship's captain, unable to find replacements for two sailors who deserted the ship, promised to divide the deserters' wages among the remaining crew if they would sail the ship home. The court decided that the promise was unenforceable because of the lack of consideration. In sailing the ship home, the crew had done that which they were already required to do. Their original contract required them to meet the normal emergencies of the voyage, which included minor desertions. However, if there were something new in the second promise which was not required under the previous contract, (e.g., faster or better performance, a different form of performance, or performing under unusually difficult circumstances), this new undertaking may be new consideration. In the case of *Hartley v Ponsonby* (1857) 7 E&B 872, seventeen sailors out of a crew of 36 deserted the ship. The remaining 19 men sailed the ship home on the promise that they would receive greater compensation. The court held that the voyage was dangerous due to the reduced number of crew. The sailors could have refused to undertake the journey, as it went beyond the normal circumstances of a sea voyage. Therefore, the promise was binding as the plaintiff had gone beyond his duty, agreeing to sail home a dangerously undermanned ship.

Similarly, the payment of a smaller sum will not settle in full a debt for a larger amount, unless the debtor pays consideration for a new agreement to provide that the smaller payment is full payment of the debt. The reason is that the existing duty to pay the full debt remains. To provide consideration for settlement, the debtor must agree to some new obligation, such as making payment at a different time than originally agreed, or making payment at a different location than originally agreed.

In the case of *Foakes v Beer* (1884) 9 App Cas 605, Mrs. Beer obtained a judgment against Dr. Foakes in an amount over £2,090. Dr. Foakes agreed to pay £500 immediately and £150 every six months until the whole amount was paid, and Mrs. Beer agreed not to take further action on the judgment. Dr. Foakes duly paid the amount of the judgment. However, judgment debts carry interest according to the law. Thus, while Dr. Foakes had been paying off the debt, interest amounting to £360 had been accruing on the outstanding balance. In another lawsuit, Mrs. Beer claimed the £360. The court held she could do so as Dr. Foakes paid no consideration for her promise not to take further action on the judgment.

The rule that performance of an existing duty is insufficient consideration has an exception. In the case of *Williams v Roffey Bros* [1991] 1 QB 1, the defendant building contractor subcontracted carpentry works to the plaintiff for a certain amount. The plaintiff's sum was too low and the plaintiff began to experience financial difficulties. The defendant feared that there might be a delay to the works which would make the defendant liable for damages under the main contract. Therefore the defendant promised to, but did not, make extra payments to the plaintiff. The plaintiff sued for the extra payments. The court decided that the defendant received certain benefits: actual performance of the earlier contract, avoidance of the penalty for delay, and avoiding the inconvenience of engaging a substitute contractor. These benefits were sufficient consideration for the promise of extra payments. The court stated:

- if A has entered into a contract with B to do work for, or to supply goods or services to, B in return for payment by B; and
- at some stage before A has completely performed his obligations under the contract B has reason to doubt whether A will, or will be able to, complete his side of the bargain; and
- B thereupon promises A an additional payment in return for A's promise to perform his contractual obligations on time; and

- as a result of giving his promise, B obtains in practice a benefit, or obviates a disbenefit; and
- B's promise is not given as a result of economic duress[40] or fraud on the part of A; then
- the benefit to B is capable of being consideration for B's promise so that the promise will be legally binding.[41]

This case appears to be contrary to the decision in *Stilk v Myrick* and is controversial.[42] Some have suggested that if a party improperly refuses to perform its contractual obligations unless for extra payments, the refusal would amount to economic duress and the promise for extra payments would not be enforceable. However there is no suggestion of duress in *Williams*. In such a circumstance there is nothing objectionable in enforcing the promise, since this is in line with commercial reality.

Williams v Roffey Bros has been applied in Hong Kong in *UBC (Construction) Ltd v Sung Foo Kee Ltd* [1993] 2 HKLR 207. In the *UBC (Construction) Ltd* case, the contractor claimed it owed no additional monies to the plastering subcontractor for variation orders at the Wah Ming Estate because the disputed work was required under the contract rather than work which varied from the original work. According to the contractor, the disputed work thus fell within the contracted sum. There would be no consideration for agreeing to pay the subcontractor a higher sum than the contract sum. The court stated:

> An agreement to pay an additional sum for no extra work may not always fail for [lack of] consideration. When a sub-contract carpenter was in financial difficulties and the agreed price for his work was too low, it was held that there was consideration for the main contractor's promise to pay an additional amount for the same work in that the main contractor thereby secured benefits or obviated disbenefits from the continuing relationship with the sub-contractor. The benefits were:
>
> 1. seeking to ensure that the sub-contractor did not stop work in breach of contract;
> 2. avoiding the penalty for delay; and
> 3. avoiding the trouble and expense of engaging others to complete the work.[43]

On the other hand, the application of the *Williams* case is limited. In the case of *Re Selectmove* [1995] 2 All ER 531, the English Court of Appeal refused to extend the principle in *Williams* to the context of *Foakes v Beer*, namely to the part payment of a debt.

iv. Equitable Estoppel

Equitable estoppel is a legal doctrine, which permits a defendant to plead equity,[44] as a defence in order to prevent the plaintiff from enforcing its legal rights under a contract.[45] The basis for this defence is that equity will not allow a plaintiff to enforce legal rights,[46] where the plaintiff makes a statement that caused the defendant to suppose that the plaintiff would not enforce those legal rights.[47] In other words, the plaintiff gives a promise not to enforce some pre-existing right. The defendant, relying on this promise, changes its position to its detriment (i.e., disadvantage, harm or injury). Thus, this doctrine prevents a plaintiff breaching its promise by seeking to enforce its legal rights where the other party has acted on the promise and where it would be unfair or inequitable to allow the promisor to enforce the legal rights.[48] Note, however, that a court has complete discretion as to whether or not this equitable defence can be raised.

In the case of *Central London Property Trust Ltd v High Trees House Ltd* [1947] KB 130, the plaintiff in 1937 granted the defendant a ninety-nine-year lease for a new block of flats at a rent of £2,500 per annum. During World War II, the flats were not fully let as many people had left London to avoid being bombed by the Nazis. The defendant realised that it could not meet the rent payments owed to the plaintiff from the profits then being made on the flats. Consequently, in 1940 the parties agreed to reduce the rent to £1,250 per annum. This agreement was in writing but not sealed. The defendant paid the reduced rent from 1941 to the beginning of 1945, by which time the flats were fully let. The defendant continued to pay the reduced rent thereafter. In September 1945, the plaintiff asked for arrears of £7,916, claiming that the liability created by the 1937 lease still existed, and that there was no consideration or any seal for the 1940 agreement. The court decided that as the defendant had acted upon the rent reduction agreement, the plaintiff was estopped in equity from claiming the full rent from 1941 until early 1945 when the flats were fully let. After that time the plaintiff was entitled to the original rent because the second agreement only applied during the conditions which gave rise to it, i.e., World War II. To this extent, the claim succeeded. If the plaintiff had sued for the balance of rent from 1941, its case would have failed.

For equitable estoppel to apply, there must be both inducement (some type of enticement or lure) by the plaintiff and detrimental reliance by the defendant.[49] There must be evidence to show that the plaintiff actually intended the defendant to act on the promise, or that it was reasonable for the defendant to do so. The form of reliance must have been reasonable or intended. The detriment suffered by the defendant is measured at the time when the plaintiff proposes to deny the promise or withdraw the promise, rather than at the time when the denial or withdrawal was made. Further, the behaviour of the plaintiff must be unconscionable. The promise must have caused the defendant to act in such a way that it would be inequitable for the plaintiff to change its mind. In determining whether the plaintiff acted unconscionably, the courts will examine a number of factors: the nature of the inducement, the content of the representation, the relative knowledge of the parties, the parties' relative strength in their bargaining positions, the pre-existing relationship (if any between the parties), the parties' relative interest in the relevant activities in reliance, and any protective measure taken by either party.

In summation, in order to raise the defence of equitable estoppel:

- there must be an original agreement between the parties by which the defendant owed an obligation to the plaintiff;
- the plaintiff, by words or conduct, must have waived its rights under the original agreement;
- the defendant may have given no consideration for the plaintiff's promises;
- the defendant has changed its position in reliance on the plaintiff's promises; and
- allowance of the insistence on the terms of the original agreement by the plaintiff would be inequitable.

As an equitable remedy, promissory estoppel will not apply where a party seeking to rely upon this doctrine has not acted fairly or equitably.[50]

v. Accord and Satisfaction

Accord refers to an agreement. *Satisfaction* refers to consideration. Thus, accord and satisfaction is an agreement, with consideration, for the payment of a debt, in instances where the amount of debt is not readily ascertainable, not agreed upon or disputed in good faith. Accord and satisfaction is the purchase, using valuable consideration, of a release from an obligation. The accord is the agreement by which the original obligation is paid off, or by which the original debt is substituted with a new amount. The accord does not cancel the debt but merely suspends it until the accord is fully performed. If the debtor fails to perform the accord, the other party can elect to enforce the terms of original contract, or to sue under terms of the accord. The satisfaction is the consideration which gives effect to the agreement, the full performance of the new agreement.[51]

For there to be accord and satisfaction for payment of a debt for less than the full amount owed, a debtor must provide a creditor with something of additional value or suffer some additional detriment.[52] Otherwise, the original contract and debt remains.

Examples of consideration in an accord and satisfaction situation include instances where:

- the debtor makes early payment upon the creditor's request;
- the debtor makes payment at a different place at the creditor's request;
- the method of payment is changed; or
- the debtor gives some chattel of value together with a reduced cash payment.[53]

Accord does not exist if a creditor is forced to accept a lesser sum than the amount of indebtedness, as was the situation in the case of *D & C Builders Ltd v Rees* [1966] 2 QB 617. D & C Builders did work for Mr. Rees. Initially, no dispute arose as to the quality of the work but Mr. Rees failed to pay. In August and October 1964, the plaintiffs received no reply to their requests for payment. In November 1964, during Mr. Rees' illness, his wife telephoned the plaintiffs, complaining about the quality of the work. She offered £300 as full payment. D & C Builders, faced with bankruptcy without payment of the whole of the original amount, offered to accept the £300 and allow payment of the balance within a year. Mrs. Rees rejected this proposal, indicating that £300 was better than no payment. The plaintiffs considered that they had no choice but to accept. Later, the plaintiffs, concerned over their financial position, sued for the unpaid amount. The Reeses claimed there was a binding settlement. The court decided that payment of a smaller sum in cash could not be settlement of a larger sum.

An exception is where a third party pays a smaller sum which is accepted by the creditor as full payment of the debtor's larger debt. The creditor cannot subsequently sue the debtor for the balance because otherwise it would be a fraud on the third party. For example, Alan owed $500 to Bill but Alan cannot repay this amount in full. Cindy proposes an agreement with Bill to repay $300 of Alan's debt. In return for Cindy's payment, Bill is to consider Alan's debt as paid in full. If Bill agrees to this proposal, Bill cannot accept Cindy's $300 and still sue Alan for the remaining $200.

Another exception is that where a debtor reaches a compromise[54] agreement with a number of creditors at the same time, no single creditor is entitled to return to its strict legal rights.[55] This is an important exception to the rule that an agreement where a creditor accepts part payment of the debt in full satisfaction of the amount owed does not discharge the whole debt. A composition with creditors may arise where there is an agreement between the debtor and some or all of the creditors. Under this agreement, the creditors agree with the debtor, and with each other, to accept the debtor's payment of less than the full amounts due to the creditors in full satisfaction of the whole of their claims. Such an agreement is binding on all parties. If the debtor complies with its obligations under the accord, then the original debt is discharged.[56]

A final exception concerns a settlement agreement under seal. In this situation, there would be no requirement for consideration. The general rule is that a contract must be supported by consideration unless it was made under seal.[57] A seal thus takes the place of consideration.[58] A *contract under seal* is a document to which the maker's seal is attached and which is delivered as his deed.[59] However, a contract under seal but without any consideration may not take advantage of certain remedies in the event of a breach,[60] such as specific performance or an injunction.[61] This type of contract is discussed in detail in Chapter 2, section F.

A case from the United Kingdom demonstrates the application of promissory estoppel to a situation apparently involving accord and satisfaction. *Collier v P & M J Wright (Holdings) Ltd* [2008] 1 WLR 643 seems to contradict the court decision in *Foakes v Beer*. Unlike the outcome in the *Foakes* case, the *Collier* court appears to extend the application of promissory estoppel by finding that relying upon a creditor's promise not to sue for the full debt makes the creditor's failure to fulfil that promise inequitable. *Collier* involved three business partners jointly liable to Wright. Following the partners' bankruptcy, Wright attempted to collect the total partnership debt solely from Collier. Collier argued that as Wright had promised not to pursue Collier for the full amount of the partnership debt, Collier should be able to rely upon this promise. The court decided that unlike the decision in *Foakes*, partial payment of a debt will discharge the whole debt amount if the partial payment was made in response to the creditor's agreement or promise that the partial payment would satisfy the whole outstanding amount. The court in *Collier* concluded that:

1. if a debtor offers to pay only a portion of the amount owed;
2. the creditor accepts that offer;
3. in reliance upon the creditor's acceptance, the debtor pays that agreed portion of the amount owed; and
4. the creditor, by the application of promissory estoppel, will be prevented from pursuing the debtor for the outstanding balance of the debt.[62]

This court decision applies only to the UK and it is yet unknown whether Hong Kong courts would follow this precedent. Nonetheless, the *Collier* case may be considered as an example of the ever-evolving common law.

4

Contents

This chapter is concerned with the contents or provisions of a contract. Thus, this chapter will discuss the matters concerning the obligations and responsibilities of the parties in the legally binding agreement based upon its provisions.

A. Certainty of Terms

Before reviewing the provisions of an agreement, courts need to determine whether the agreement is a legally enforceable contract. Recall the earlier discussion concerning the elements of a legally binding agreement. One of these requirements for a contract is *certainty*. In other words, a contract requires sufficient details before the agreement can be enforced legally. A contract cannot contain too many unknown features affecting matters such as quantity, price, place of delivery, time of delivery, payment methods, etc. This section discusses the need for certainty of terms in order to have a legally enforceable agreement.

The parties to a contract undertake obligations and obtain certain rights as defined in the provisions of their contract. These provisions may be expressed or implied. These provisions, however, must not be so vague, uncertain or ambiguous that a court is unable to apply them. If a court cannot apply or enforce the agreement's provisions, the contract is void for uncertainty. The general rule is that the courts will interpret a contract according to the parties' intentions at the time the contract was made.

> The general rule is that, if the terms of an agreement are so vague or indefinite that it cannot be ascertained with reasonable certainty what is the intention of the parties, there is no contract enforceable at law. This may happen in two ways: a clause may be devoid of any

> meaning or have such a wide variety of meanings that it is impossible to say which of them is intended. . . .
>
> The courts, however, do not expect commercial documents to be drafted with strict precision; the court will look at the document as a whole . . . in construing an agreement, a court should not hold a provision to be void for uncertainty unless it cannot resolve the ambiguity . . . Finally, it should be remembered that the degree of uncertainty in an agreement is a factor which may go to the question of whether or not the parties intend to create legal relations.[1]

The case of *Professional Associates v Polytek Engineering Co Ltd* [1986] HKLR 20 involved the issue of the existence of a contract between an architectural firm and several companies proposing a hotel construction project in the People's Republic of China. The joint venture company responsible for the actual construction project had yet to be created and the approval of Mainland officials had yet to be obtained. The Hong Kong High Court, in deciding the existence of a contract, discussed the element of certainty by referring to the case of *G Scammell and Nephew Ltd v H C and J G Ouston* [1941] AC 251. The Hong Kong High Court stated:

> that in order for a contract to be binding the terms must be so definite that no further agreement is necessary between the parties to render them certain . . . As a matter of law the contract price must be certain. But certainty may be achieved by more than one route. The common and simple alternative is for an express fixed contract sum to be stipulated. However, the contract price is equally certain if instead of an express fixed sum, a formula is agreed upon under which the contract price may be ascertained, without further agreement by the parties.[2]

B. Contractual Provisions

Once the certainty of terms is found to exist and assuming all the other elements are present, the next step is to examine these terms for their meaning or intent. This is because the provisions of a contract define the obligations and the rights of the parties to that contract.

> Assuming that a contract has been validly created, it is necessary to consider the extent of the obligations imposed on the parties by the contract. In order to do this, the exact terms of the contract must be determined and their comparative importance evaluated.[3]

Thus, as discussed in the preceding section, the provisions of a contract must be sufficiently certain or definite so as to be enforceable in court.

In this section, we review how a court may interpret and apply those provisions.

The provisions of a contract are frequently disputed as each party claims a different interpretation of a particular provision. For example, in the case of *Pacific Dunlop Garments Ltd v Fundamental Global Ltd* [2014] HKEC 609, the dispute involved the interpretation of the phrase 'unacceptable risks . . . to the Purchaser'. Specifically, the parties disagreed over whether this phrase should be determined subjectively or objectively. The Court of Appeal quoted the decision of the trial court judge who said:

> Different people or companies must have different attitude to risks taking. For a company, any risks taking decision must depend on a host of factors, e.g., financial ability, the return, the business plan and the ethos of the management. I simply cannot see how acceptability of risks can be assessed with a notional reasonable company. What are the attributes of this reasonable company? Is the court to assume that the management is conservative or adventurous or somewhere in the middle, and what does it mean when the management is neither conservative nor adventurous?[4]

The Court of Appeal continued:

> In my judgment, the reasoning of the judge . . . is plainly correct. Effect must be given to the clear wording of the provision that one is concerned with "unacceptable risks to . . . the Purchaser". I see no basis to water down the subjective element by grafting on to this an objective standard.[5]

In the case of *Fully Profit (Asia) Ltd v Secretary for Justice* (2013) 16 HKCFAR 351, the Court of Final Appeal was asked to interpret the word 'house' in relation to a government land restriction that no more than one house can be erected on each lot. Fully Profit wanted to erect a single 26-storey building straddling five adjacent lots. This building would have shops and facilities on the two lower floors and residential flats on the remaining twenty-four floors. The Court of Final Appeal stated:

> What emerges from these cases—and other authorities on contractual interpretation—is the overall importance of context when construing contractual terms. The statements of principle in *Investors Compensation Scheme* and in *Jumbo King* refer time and again to the relevant background against which the relevant contract and contractual terms must be viewed. It is in my view not particularly helpful in most cases to refer to the "ordinary and natural meaning"

> of words because, as very often experience tells us, there can be much debate over exactly what is the ordinary or natural meaning of words. The surer guide to interpretation is context. . . . Here, I would just add that in the area of statutory and constitutional interpretation, it is context that is key; context is the starting point (together with purpose) rather than looking at what may be the natural and ordinary meaning of words.[6]

If the interpretation of a particular provision is not in dispute, the category of the provision might determine the type and amount of recovery an injured party may receive or the consequences a party may face for failing to fulfil its legal obligations.

To explain the legal principles more clearly, we will use the following scenario: Alice, a very rich *tai tai*, enters a shop seeking a refrigerator for a new designer home on the Peak into which Alice will move in 30 days. In 40 days, Alice will host an open-house party to show off her new home to her rich and influential friends. After long discussions with a shop's sales consultant, Alice enters into a contract with the shop for the purchase of a black Sub-Zero® brand of refrigerator for Alice's new home. What was said during those discussions? Did the sales consultant make any statements (known as *representations*) which influenced Alice's decision to buy the Sub-Zero® refrigerator rather than a Samsung® refrigerator? Did any portions of the discussions between Alice and the sales consultant become part of the contract? What are the consequences if the shop:

- delivers a yellow and purple coloured model?
- delivers a black Samsung® refrigerator?
- delivers a black Sub-Zero® refrigerator that has a scratch on the side which will be hidden once the refrigerator is installed in the cabinetry?
- delivers the correct product later than agreed?

i. Expressed and Implied Terms

A contract's provisions may be placed into several categories. The contents of a contract may be placed in the category of expressed or implied term. An *express term* is an expressed promise which forms an integral part of the contract. Even such a simple concept can have difficulties on application:

> [W]here there is such a contractual document, it by no means follows that that document will contain all the terms agreed between the parties. Leaving aside the possibility of implied terms, there may be (1) express oral terms, for most contracts may be made wholly or partly by word of mouth; or (2) a collateral contract.

> Where there is a contractual document, the question whether the agreement between the parties contains additional, or even contradictory, oral terms is one of fact, to be decided by extrinsic evidence. Once all the express terms of a contract have been ascertained, their meaning is a matter of construction.[7]

An *implied term* is a term which the parties intended and which they would have included expressly if they had thought about this issue of its inclusion at the time of contracting.[8]

> Custom and usage may be used by the court to add an implied term. The rationale is that the parties did not express all of the terms of the agreement but only those necessary for this particular case; relying on regular trade customs and practices to complete the remainder of the terms. As the courts are reluctant to imply such terms, the person arguing in favour of the inclusion of such a term has to show that the custom is well-established in that particular trade, industry or locality. The implied term must be consistent with any express term as it is within the parties' powers to expressly exclude any customary term.[9]

In order for a Hong Kong court to imply term(s) into a contract, the term(s) should be:

- reasonable and equitable;
- necessary to give effect to the contract (known as *business efficacy*);
- so obvious that it 'goes without saying';
- capable of clear expression; and
- consistent with, and not contradict, any express term of the contract.[10]

These guidelines have been followed recently by the Court of Appeal in the case of *Hua Ning Industries Ltd v Best Leader Engineering Ltd* [2014] HKEC 228 and by the Court of First Instance in the case of *Wan Chi Hing v Wong Chung Kai* [2015] HKEC 1241.

Parties may insert a *merger clause* into the agreement to indicate to the courts that the written terms are the complete agreement. A merger clause is intended to prevent one party from attempting to later supplement the contract with terms that were not originally included in the contract.

ii. Conditions and Warranties

Previously, we stated that a contract's provisions may be placed into several categories. The provisions in a contract may also be classified under the category of *condition*[11] or under the category of *warranty*.[12] In the case of *The Moorcock* (1889) 14 PD 64, the court determined that the word *conditions* refers to the significant provisions of a contract. A *condition* is a term which goes to the basis or foundation of the contract, to the whole of the consideration. A *warranty* refers to a less important provision of a contract. A warranty is only part of the consideration.

> The predominant modern approach is to consider the nature of the terms of the contract in order to decide whether those terms are conditions or warranties. . . . a breach of condition entitles the innocent party to rescind the contract and claim damages for any loss he may have suffered, whereas a breach of warranty only entitles him to damages.[13]

Failure to act by an agreed date, or to meet a time requirement in a contract, is usually not a material or substantial breach of the contract. However, if the date fixed in the contract is expressly made *time is of the essence* by the parties, the failure to comply with this stipulation is a material breach. If the contract does not contain a deadline, the time for performance is whatever will be reasonable under the circumstances. An unreasonable delay in performance can be a material breach. In determining the reasonableness of the time of performance, the court will examine:

- the parties' intent;
- whether the parties have acted in good faith; and
- any hardship to the innocent party caused by the failure to fulfil the contract in time.

As will be further discussed later in this section, the present approach of the courts to evaluating contract provisions is to consider another category. This third category of contract provisions is known as an *intermediate* term or *innominate* term. *Innominate* means without a name.[14] A term is likely to be classified as *intermediate* if it is capable of being breached either:

- in a manner that is trivial and capable of remedy by a payment of damages, or
- in a manner that is so fundamental as to undermine the whole contract.[15]

This topic of intermediate term will be analysed in more detail in section viii. Depending upon the type and the consequences of a breach, the innocent party may or may not be discharged from the contract.[16]

iii. Representations

A *representation* is the title given to a statement made to tempt or to persuade a party into making a contract.[17] Representations are not part of the contract and the legal consequences are different. Accordingly, determining the difference between a statement which is a condition and one which is a representation becomes necessary.

> Basically, the problem is one of determining the intention of the parties as evidenced by their words and conduct, so that no general principle of interpretation can be universally true. Because, however, the intention of the parties seldom clearly appears, the courts have had regard to any one or more of a number of factors for attributing an intention.[18]

iv. Puff

Puff refers to statements which neither party takes seriously. Puff may be considered to be the equivalent of the sales pitch made by a sales clerk to entice a customer to make a purchase.[19] Puff does not have any legal force.

> A notable example in Hong Kong relates to estate agents' advertising where it is generally accepted that descriptions should not be taken literally. Attempts to sell new properties on the Pok Fu Lam coast may feature photographs of apartments on the Mediterranean with the justification that what is being indicated is a 'concept'. Such behaviour is so widespread that it is fair to say that few Hong Kong people would take the images seriously. This view was given judicial support in *Chan Yeuk Yu & Another v Church Body of the Hong Kong Sheng Kung Hui & Another* where Burrell J, dealing with the words 'regal surroundings for the select few' stated:
>
> > taken in its context, namely on page 4 of a 27-page glossy and colourful sales brochure, I find it difficult to conclude that it is any more than "mere puff" or "sales pitch".[20]

v. Factors of Classifications

Whether a statement is a term (either a condition or a warranty), representation, or puff depends upon the parties' intentions. Thus, it becomes important to determine what the parties intended a statement to be. Some guidelines are available to assist in classifying these statements:

- Time: If a statement was made at the beginning of long negotiations and not repeated, it is likely to be a representation. If a statement was made repeatedly or emphasised near the conclusion of negotiations, it is likely to be a term.

- Importance: Occasionally, this criterion overlaps with the time guideline. If a statement is made at the beginning of negotiations and not mentioned again, it is likely to be a representation. However, if a statement sets the basis of negotiations, it may be a term. For example, if great stress was placed upon a particular aspect of the negotiations, that matter may become a term.[21]
- Expertise of parties: A statement made by a person with special knowledge is more likely to be a term.
- Writing: In a written contract, the document is presumed to contain all the terms; any omitted statements are presumed to be representations.

vi. Effects of Classification

A statement's classification is important when there is a breach of the contract. The classification determines the remedies available to the innocent party for any loss resulting from the breach:

- Breach of a contractual term may result in damages or specific performance.[22] A breach of condition results in the innocent party having the right to end the agreement as well as the right to sue for damages. Should the innocent party end the contract, the innocent party does not need to fulfil its own obligations under the agreement. Additionally, the innocent party may keep any benefit, as long as the agreement was ended and notice given of the termination within a reasonable time. In addition, the innocent party may sue for damages for the loss suffered. Alternatively, the innocent party may continue with the contract rather than end the agreement. In such a case, the innocent party may also sue for damages, treating the breach of condition as a breach of warranty. A breach of a warranty results in the innocent party having the right to claim damages; the innocent party has no right to terminate the contract.
- Misrepresentation may result in rescission under the common law or in damages under statutory law.
- Puff which is untrue does not allow recovery.

vii. Determining Classification

The general rule is that courts will interpret a contract according to the parties' intentions at the time the contract was made. 'The contract is to be construed so as to find and give effect to the intentions of the parties to it.'[23]

Intention is to be found from the contract itself upon a proper construction of its terms as a whole, according to the decision in *Suisse Atlantique Société d'Armement Maritime SA v NV Rotterdamsche Kolen Centrale* [1967] AC 361. As one authority has noted:

> The cardinal presumption is that the words of the agreement mean what the parties have in fact said, so that their words must be construed as they stand. . . . the meaning of the document or of a particular part of it is to be sought *in the document itself*: "[o]ne must consider the meaning of the words used, not what one may guess to be the intention of the parties". However, this is not to say that the meaning of the words in a written document must be ascertained by reference to the words of the document alone. The courts will . . . look at all the circumstances surrounding the making of the contract . . . which would assist in determining how the language of the document would have been understood by a reasonable person in their position.
>
> Further it has long been accepted that the courts will not approach the task of construction with too nice a concentration upon individual words.[24]

Additionally, in matters concerning the interpretation of a contract, note the *contra proferentem*[25] rule which states that courts will interpret any ambiguous contract provisions against the party who drafted the agreement.

> *Contra* means against, and *proferentem* is a neat way of referring to the person relying on the document – that is, the drafter of it, the *proferens*. Any ambiguities are construed against the *proferens*. That is, the drafter never gets the benefit of any doubt.[26]

The purpose of a judicial interpretation of contract provisions is to determine the importance which the contracting parties had attached to these terms. This classification then assists in determining the consequences of a breach of those contract provisions, because the type of breach determines the remedies available to the innocent party.

The seriousness of the results of a breach should serve as the determining factor in whether the breach was fundamental or minor.[27] If the breach is determined to be fundamental, the innocent party may treat its obligations under that contract as ended or discharged and may also sue for damages. If the breach is considered to be minor, neither party may consider their obligations under that contract to be discharged until performance is completed. A court, however, will still award damages upon proof of the breach.

viii. Intermediate Term

The case of *Hong Kong Fir Shipping Co v Kawasaki Kisen Kaisha* [1962] 2 QB 26 sets out the current approach towards using the intermediate (also known as *innominate*) term to interpret the provisions of a contract. Rather than automatically classifying the breach as one of condition or of warranty, the use of the innominate term seeks to be flexible. This approach recognises that the remedy for the breach will depend on the effect of the breach. This test considers all factors, including the circumstances of the breach, to determine whether a party has been deprived of the contract's benefits. If the answer is *yes*, the breach is treated as a breach of condition. If the answer is *no*, the breach is treated as a breach of warranty.[28] Thus, the result of the interpretation depends on the breach's consequences rather than following automatically from a prior classification as a condition or as a warranty.

In *Hong Kong Fir Shipping*, the defendants hired a ship for 24 months from February 1957 under an agreement which provided: 'She [the ship] being in every way fitted for ordinary cargo service.' The owners also agreed to maintain the ship 'in a thoroughly efficient state'. Upon delivery, the ship's engine room was undermanned and the staff incompetent. Upon the ship's arrival at one destination in May 1957, the defendants discovered that the ship required repairs which would take 15 weeks. The defendants wrote to the ship owners in June 1957 cancelling the agreement because of the owners' breaches of contract, claiming the failure to provide a seaworthy ship and the negligent failure to maintain the ship in a proper state. The ship became seaworthy in September 1957. The court determined that the breaches did not entitle the defendants to cancel the contract since neither the unseaworthiness nor the delay entitled them to do so. The unseaworthiness and failure to maintain were not breaches of conditions. Furthermore, the delay had not hindered the venture's commercial purpose.

One reason for this outcome is because courts hesitate to allow a party to cancel a contract in order to avoid a bad bargain. It appears that the defendants in *Hong Kong Fir Shipping* attempted to cancel the contract because freight rates had fallen since the commencement of the contract and the defendants could have hired other ships less expensively. However, the evidence showed that the defendants had not suffered any loss because, while the ship was being repaired, the defendants were not required to pay hire for the ship. Furthermore, during the repair period, the defendants could have sent the goods at lower freight rates. Consequently, the defendants' commercial purpose was not harmed.

In the case of *Cehave NV v Bremer Handelsgesellschaft mbH (The Hansa Nord)* [1976] 1 QB 44 the defendants sold citrus pulp pellets to the plaintiffs. A contract provision stated 'shipment to be made in good condition'. The goods were delivered in several batches, and when a particular batch arrived at Rotterdam the price of the goods had fallen. Of the total of 3,293 tonnes, 1,260 tonnes were damaged. The plaintiffs rejected the whole 3,293 tonnes on the basis that the shipment was not made in good condition and claimed for the price of the goods (£100,000). A middleman purchased the goods for £33,720 and resold them to the plaintiffs at that price. The plaintiffs used the pellets to make cattle food, as originally intended. This transaction resulted in the plaintiffs receiving goods for which they had agreed to pay £100,000 at the reduced price of £33,720. The court decided in favour of the sellers. The court held that the contractual term 'shipment to be made in good condition' was not a condition, but rather was an intermediate term. As the court said:

> If a small portion of the whole cargo was not in good condition and arrived a little unsound, it should be met by a price allowance. The buyer should not have the right to reject the whole lot unless the divergence was serious or substantial.[29]

C. Exclusion Clauses

In the preceding sections, we discussed the consequences of a breach of contract: what is a breach, what are the different types of breach, and what are the results or consequences of the breach. In this section, we review the ways in which a party might attempt to avoid liability for a breach of contract.

Because of the liability involved in a breach of contract, parties have attempted to limit or waive their liability through the use of a *limitation clause*, which is also known as an *exclusion clause* or *exemption clause*.[30] Although there are different names for contractual clauses which attempt to limit liability, they are quite similar in purpose:

> Though 'exemption clause' is perhaps the most popular, clauses attempting to restrict liability have many names. 'Limitation clause' is the term usually used to indicate that remedies have been cut down, not out completely. Typically, such a clause will say that

> claims will be restricted in type or amount. . . . A laundry may accept your clothes only on terms that they will be liable for $100 or the full amount of the loss – whichever is the less. . . .
>
> An 'exclusion clause' suggests that no claim will be entertained. For example, the words 'No responsibility is taken for any loss, damage or injury howsoever caused' may be found on a notice at the entrance to a car park. They clearly envisage that you will have no claim at all.
>
> 'Exception clause' is sometimes used instead of 'exemption', but does not seem to have any different meaning. You can normally use exemption or exception clause to mean a limitation or exclusion clause.[31]

As previously stated, exclusion clauses excuse a party from liability which may arise from a contract. The parties may include a provision which excludes liability for a specified breach or which limits liability in some way. The courts are careful in interpreting such clauses and enforce them only if expressed in clear language. Courts do so because such clauses deny legal remedies to the injured party. If an exclusion clause can be invalidated or its application restricted, a court will often do so on public policy[32] grounds. Public policy does not like one party contracting away liability for conduct that disregards the rights of others, or for intentional torts or gross negligence.

Under the common law, limitation clauses must be strictly proved. Courts may use this requirement with the *contra proferentem* rule to restrict the application of limitation clauses. Recall that the *contra proferentem* rule of interpretation allows courts to interpret any ambiguity of an exemption clause against the party who inserted the clause and who wants to rely on this clause.[33]

Where an exemption clause is contained in an unsigned document and/or notice, the following factors are important to determine the clause's applicability:

- Did the document or notice form part of the contract? It is, thus, important to determine how and when the contract was made; the offer and acceptance approach may assist in making this determination. For example, a ticket which comes as a receipt, after the contract is made, cannot be part of that contract and cannot impose contractual terms. In another example, a notice on the inside of a hotel room door cannot exclude the hotel from its liability for negligence. Why is this so? The answer is that the guest's registration takes place at the front desk, well before a guest enters the hotel room and sees the notice.

- Even where the document or notice is part of the contract, there may be a question whether the other party knew of the clause. Unless there was clear notice of the exclusion clause when the contract was made, and assuming no previous dealings between these parties or assuming no basis for implying knowledge, a court will usually find the exclusion clause to be invalid. What forms sufficient notice is a question of fact for a court to determine, but the more unusual the terms of an exclusion clause, the more explicit the warning must be.
- Where the parties have previous dealings, the exclusion clause usually could be considered part of the contract. The reason is that notice only applies where there is a lack of knowledge of the contract terms. A history of prior dealings implies knowledge of the contract provisions.[34]

The case of *Thornton v Shoe Lane Parking Ltd* [1971] 2 QB 163 demonstrates the application of some of the above rules. The plaintiff upon entering the car park paid a fee and then received a ticket. On the back side of the ticket was a clause excluding liability for personal injuries to customers. The plaintiff was injured and sued the defendant who relied upon the exclusion clause. The court determined that this exclusion clause came too late to be part of the contract. As the court stated:

> The customer pays his money and gets a ticket. He cannot refuse it. He cannot get his money back. He may protest to the machine, even swear at it. But it will remain unmoved. He is committed beyond recall. He was committed at the very moment when he put his money into the machine. The contract was concluded at that time. It can be translated into offer and acceptance in this way: the offer is made when the proprietor of the machine holds it out as being ready to receive the money. The acceptance takes place when the customer puts his money into the slot. The terms of the offer are contained in the notice placed on or near the machine stating what is offered for the money. The customer is bound by those terms as long as they are sufficiently brought to his notice before-hand but not otherwise. He is not bound by the terms printed on the ticket if they differ from the notice, because the ticket comes too late.[35]

Exemption clauses in signed documents are treated differently. The general rule is that a party who signs a document is bound. A party is assumed to know the contents of a document that the party signed.[36] An example of an effective exemption clause may be found in the case of *Ying Wei (Hop Yick) Cargo Service v Nanyang Credit Card Co Ltd* [1993]

1 HKC 56. The defendant contracted to hoist the plaintiff's computer equipment up to its offices on the fifth floor of a building. During the hoisting operation, the computer equipment fell to the fourth floor, damaging the equipment. The contract between the parties provided that 'price not included [*sic*] insurance charges', that insurance against damage should be covered by Nanyang Credit Card Co Ltd, and that 'not [*sic*] damage claim to our company for this hoisting operation'.

The credit card company sued and the defendant relied on the exemption clause. The credit card company argued that:

- the term 'hoisting operation' was unclear and should only cover a proper hoisting operation, i.e., without negligence;
- the term 'not damage claim' was not clear and should cover only pure consequential or economic loss as opposed to physical damage to the equipment itself; and
- the clause itself was unclear because it was not grammatical and not even a sentence.

The court rejected these arguments, determining that the exemption clause was clear enough to exempt any damage claim against the defendant in respect of the hoisting operation even if interpreted *contra proferentem* against the defendant. Although the clause did not expressly exclude liability based on negligence, the court stated that 'it is difficult to see that the parties could not have had in mind primarily claims for negligence'.[37] This view is reinforced by the fact that the contract required the plaintiff to buy insurance.

Under legislation, certain restrictions may be placed upon the effect of exemption clauses. Other jurisdictions have enacted a variety of laws to limit the application of exclusion clauses, particularly in consumer contracts. In Hong Kong, statutory control of such clauses is minimal. The major law controlling exemption clauses is contained in the Control of Exemption Clauses Ordinance (Cap 71) which states its purpose as being '[t]o limit the extent to which civil liability for breach of contract, or for negligence or other breach of duty, can be avoided by means of contract terms'.[38]

This law generally applies to business liability. Section 2(1) defines *business* as:

> (業務) includes a profession and the activities of a public body, a public authority, or a board, commission, committee or other body appointed by the Chief Executive or Government.

Section 2(2) provides:

> In the case of both **contract** and tort, sections 7 to 12 apply . . . **only to business liability**, that is liability for breach of obligations or duties arising–
>
> (a) from **things done or omitted to be done by a person in the course of a business** (whether his own business or another's); or
>
> (b) from the occupation of premises used for business purposes of the occupier,
>
> and references to liability are to be read accordingly; but liability of an occupier of premises for breach of an obligation or duty towards a person obtaining access to the premises for recreational or educational purposes, being liability for loss or damage suffered by reason of the dangerous state of the premises, is not a business liability of the occupier unless granting that person such access for the purposes concerned falls within the business purposes of the occupier. (emphasis added)

For the purposes of this book, we will review where the provisions of this ordinance apply, that is where one of the parties enters into a contract as a consumer or using the other party's standard printed form.[39] However, for completeness, we should note that the Control of Exemption Clauses Ordinance does not apply to the following:

- contracts of insurance;
- contracts affecting the disposition of land;
- contracts concerning intellectual property;
- contracts affecting the creation or dissolution of companies; or
- contracts pertaining to the creation or transfer of securities.[40]

In situations where the Control of Exemption Clauses Ordinance does apply, the statute imposes two major restrictions upon the use of exemption provisions. The first limitation is that this law prohibits the use of exemption clauses to avoid liability for injury or death. Section 7(1) of this ordinance provides:

> A person cannot by reference to any contract term or to a notice given to persons generally or to particular persons exclude or restrict his liability for death or personal injury resulting from negligence.

The other major restriction on the use of exemption clauses pertains to the reasonableness of the exclusion.[41] In other words, in order for an exemption clause to be valid, the clause must be reasonable. The guidelines for determining reasonableness are set out in section 3 and in Schedule 2 of the statute. This test is flexible and will depend upon the facts of each case.

Further, this ordinance also prevents:

- making the liability or its enforcement subject to restrictive or onerous conditions;
- excluding or restricting any right or remedy in respect of the liability, or subjecting a person to any prejudice in consequence of his pursuing any such right or remedy; and
- excluding or restricting rules of evidence or procedure.[42]

Other examples of statutory control of exemption clauses may be found in the following:

- Sale of Goods Ordinance (Cap 26), section 57
- Misrepresentation Ordinance (Cap 284), section 4
- Supply of Services (Implied Terms) Ordinance (Cap 457), section 8

D. Void for Uncertainty

A contract is void for uncertainty where the contract terms are so vague, uncertain or ambiguous that a court cannot give clear expression to the terms. In other words, one of the required elements of a contract—the certainty of terms—is missing. Therefore, there is no legally enforceable agreement between the parties.

Courts will generally do their best to give effect to a contract, as there is a presumption that the parties intended the contract to mean something. However, courts will not make a contract for the parties. Thus, courts may imply terms based on the supposed intention of parties, or based on trade custom or from a previous history of business dealings between the parties.

The case of *David Friedman v Sieger Ltd* [2014] HKEC 44 involved a dispute over the design and fitting out of Friedman's intended residence which was under construction at the time. In reviewing the parties' dispute over the provisions of their agreement, the court stated:

> The principles concerning the implication of terms into a contract are also uncontroversial. The court will be prepared to imply a term if it represents the obvious, but unexpressed intention of the parties. In *Chitty on Contracts*, 31st ed, vol 1, [13-008] the authors summarise the position as follows:

> **Obvious inference from agreement**. A term which has not been expressed may also be implied if it was so obviously a stipulation in the agreement that the parties must have intended it to form part of their contract. . . .
>
> A term will not, however, thus be implied unless the court is satisfied that *both* parties would, as reasonable men, have agreed to it had it been suggested to them. The knowledge or ignorance of each party of the matter to be implied, or of the facts on which the implication is based, is therefore a relevant factor.[43]

If a court does not have some acceptable basis to uphold a contract, the court will not do so. Note for reference that some contract terms are implied by statute, e.g., the Sale of Goods Ordinance (Cap 26).

5

Vitiating Factors

The ways in which an otherwise legally binding agreement may be set aside (*vitiated*, i.e., made void or voidable) are discussed in this chapter.[1] The grounds for vitiating a contract commonly focus on whether there was any genuine agreement, e.g., did a party actually know what it was doing, or did a party have any real choice? Thus, this generally concerns a party's ability to enter knowingly and voluntarily into a legally binding agreement, i.e., whether there was a 'meeting of the minds' of the parties. These grounds, which centre on the required elements of capacity and consent, will be discussed first. Other grounds to vitiate a contract will be presented at the end of this chapter.

A. Capacity

This refers to the legal ability, competency, or fitness of a party to knowingly enter and be bound by a contract. Here, *party* may refer to a natural person, i.e., an individual or a group of individuals. *Party* may also refer to a legal person, i.e., a legal entity such as a company. A party to a legally binding agreement must have the ability under the law to enter into a contract.[2] Without the ability to enter into a legally binding relationship, the party is considered to lack capacity. The general rule is that the law presumes every natural person has the capacity to make a contract unless falling within one of the following legal categories:

- a minor[3]
- a person who is intoxicated
- a person who is mentally disturbed[4]

A minor may enter into a contract. The other party to this agreement, however, takes a risk that the minor may not fulfil the contract where it is for non-essential goods or for money, i.e., the contract is voidable at the choice of the minor. In Hong Kong, an exception exists under section 46 of the District Court Ordinance (Cap 336).[5] This section provides that infancy (below 18 years old) is no defence to a debt less than $60,000. However, where a contract concerns land, company shares, partnership, or is of a similar long-term or continuing nature, that contract is voidable at the minor's choice before reaching the age of 18 and for a reasonable time afterwards.[6]

A person intoxicated at the time of making a contract may lack the capacity to understand or appreciate the obligations of that legally binding agreement. Thus, this person might not have the necessary ability and/or willingness to enter into a contract. Being intoxicated does not automatically make a person incapable of entering into contracts. A person claiming intoxication at the time of contracting needs to prove two elements:

(a) Intoxication was to the level that prevented full appreciation of the nature of the contract and of the person's act in entering the agreement at the time.
(b) The other party reasonably knew that the intoxicated person was unable to act in a reasonable manner.

Similarly, to vitiate a contract on the grounds of mental disability, a person of unsound mind, through his guardian or legal representative, must prove either that:

(a) this individual was too mentally incompetent to understand the nature and consequence of entering the contract at the time, or
(b) the execution (e.g., signing) of the contract was an uncontrolled reaction to a mental illness, and the other party had reason to know of this condition.

We now consider the capacity of a legal entity, most commonly a company or business. Capacity, here, refers to the authority of a legal person, again particularly a company, to enter into contracts. A company's capacity to contract is determined by its memorandum of association and its articles of association. A company may, but is not required to, state its objects (i.e., the company's objectives or reason for existing as a business: trading company, service company, financial company, manufacturing company, construction company, etc.) in its memorandum of association. If the objects are stated, the company's power is limited by its objects. If the company enters into a contract which is outside its stated objects and if the other party has actual knowledge of the circumstances, the contract would be invalid. The other party is not considered to know of a company's capacity to contract merely because the objects are stated in the memorandum and kept by the Registrar of Companies.[7]

B. Lack of Genuine Consent

We have discussed in the preceding section that to have a valid, legally binding agreement, the parties must have the ability to enter into the contract and be able to understand the contract's obligations. Another essential requirement for a valid contract is that the parties freely agreed to accept the terms and the obligations of that agreement. In short, the parties must be able to understand the contract provisions and be able to agree to the provisions. There might not be a valid, legally binding agreement where this consent is not genuine, i.e., is not freely and voluntarily given based on full and accurate knowledge of the contract's provisions. Presented below are common situations which might prevent a party from exercising its own free will in agreeing to the contract.

When reading this section concerning genuine consent, keep in mind the situation of *tai tai* Alice and the Sub-Zero® refrigerator for her new home on the Peak mentioned in Chapter 4, section B. What representations were made by whom to whom? What was said? Was any statement(s) relied upon in making a decision? Was the relied-upon statement(s) true?

i. Misrepresentation: Generally

Misrepresentation is where an innocent party is persuaded to enter into a contract by a factual statement, upon which that party relied, and the statement was untrue.[8] If the innocent party suffered loss or damage from its reliance on that statement, remedies might be available under several situations; these will be discussed later.[9] First, however, let us discuss the requirements of misrepresentation. These requirements can be found in the definition of *misrepresentation*: a false statement of fact which causes the recipient to enter into a contract with the person making the statement.

The first element that we will review is falsehood. The statement is false. The statement must not be correct or true. Although a statement was made both honestly and reasonably, this statement, if inaccurate, may still be a misrepresentation.[10]

Another element is a statement. This requirement of a statement may consist of written words, oral statements, or conduct. For example, in the case of *Spice Girls Ltd v Aprilia World Service BV* [2000] EMLR 478 the court found an implied representation that the girl group would stay together as a singing group for the duration of the advertising contract. However, as the group knew of the pending departure of one of its members, which would affect continuation of the advertising contract, the court found there had been misrepresentation on the part of the Spice Girls even though the group had said nothing.

Thus, one of the requirements for misrepresentation is that there is a false statement. What if a party remains silent and says nothing? There is a general rule that silence will not impose liability. The following paragraphs discuss some exceptions to this general rule.

One exception is where silence is used to conceal a fact, somewhat similar to the *Spice Girls* case. Here, the concealment may be considered to be the same as saying that there is no defect. 'Covering dry rot in a house so as to conceal its existence is equivalent to a "statement" that the house is free from dry rot.'[11]

Another exception to this general rule concerns full disclosure. If a person begins to speak, the disclosure needs to be full and frank. In the case of *Dimmock v Hallett* (1866–67) LR 2 Ch App 21, the buyer of land wanted to know whether the farms on that land were leased. The seller replied 'yes'. This statement was true but the seller failed to also state that all the tenants on that land had been told to leave.[12] In this instance, the statement is literally true but is also false in the overall circumstances. The reason for this is because the statement implies other facts which are misleading or false, that is, rental income will continue to be paid by the existing tenants.

Another exception to the rule is where silence amounts to a failure to correct a previous statement. The case of *With v O'Flanagan* [1936] Ch 575 concerned the sale of a medical practice. At the beginning of negotiations, the doctor stated that his practice was worth £2000 per year. By the time the negotiations ended, the practice was worth much less due to the doctor's illness. The court found the doctor's silence to be a failure to disclose the change in the value of his medical practice. This failure to update his previous statement amounted to misrepresentation.

There is one final exception to the general rule concerning silence. This exception is known as *uberrimae fidei* (translated as *of the utmost good faith*).[13] Situations requiring *uberrimae fidei* are usually imposed by law and concern fiduciary matters such as insurance contracts, or contracts between principal and agent, and, solicitor and client relationships. In situations of *uberrimae fidei*, there is an obligation of full disclosure. Silence or partial disclosure of facts is unacceptable in *uberrimae fidei* situations.

Another required element of misrepresentation concerns whether the statement was of a fact, opinion, or intention. A false statement of a fact is misrepresentation. One should note that misrepresentation is limited to untrue statements of fact but not of opinion or intention. There would be misrepresentation of fact where a person pretends to hold an opinion which that person does not actually hold. However, if that person actually holds such an opinion which turns out to be incorrect, the representation would not be misrepresentation. Therefore, a false statement of an opinion, truly held, is not misrepresentation. An opinion may amount to a statement of fact where it can be proved that the person making the statement did not actually hold or believe in that opinion.

In the case of *Smith v Land and House Property Corp* (1884) LR 28 Ch D 7, the seller of a hotel stated that it was leased to 'a most desirable tenant' when the seller knew the tenant was frequently late in paying the rent. The court stated that: 'if the facts are not equally known to both sides, then a statement of opinion by the one who knows the facts best involves very often a statement of a material fact, for he impliedly states that he knows facts which justify his opinion'.[14] A party's statement of intention will not amount to misrepresentation should the intention change. However, a statement of intention, if not sincerely held at the time of making the statement, would be a misrepresentation of an existing fact concerning the speaker's state of mind.[15]

A further required element of misrepresentation is an inducement. The receiver of the misstatement must have been tempted or persuaded by the misstatement to enter into the contract. There would be no misrepresentation if the recipient did not receive the misstatement, ignored it, or, being aware of its falsehood, entered the contract nonetheless.

In Hong Kong, there is legislation controlling misrepresentation. This legislation is the Misrepresentation Ordinance (Cap 284) which is concerned with innocent misrepresentation. Despite this focus, certain sections of this ordinance refer to misrepresentations 'other than fraudulent'. This reference includes by inference negligent misstatement. Section 2 keeps the remedy of rescission (discussed below) for innocent misrepresentation even where the misrepresentation has become a contract term, or, where the contract has been performed.[16]

Furthermore, section 3(1) provides for damages as a remedy for non-fraudulent misrepresentation, unless the offending party proves that there had been reasonable grounds to believe that the representation was true and that the offending party believed it to be true when the contract was made. This section of the ordinance, in effect, places the burden upon the offending party to prove no misrepresentation occurred. Section 3(2) permits a court the discretion to grant damages rather than rescission. Damages may be awarded both under sections 3(1) and 3(2), but the compensation awarded under section 3(2) shall be taken into account when assessing damages under section 3(1).

Section 4 of the ordinance invalidates any exemption clause in a contract which seeks to limit remedies and liability for pre-contractual misrepresentation, except to the extent that reliance on it is considered fair and reasonable.

With the implementation of the Misrepresentation Ordinance, the general opinion is that victims of misrepresentation should bring a claim under the ordinance rather than seeking the traditional remedies available under contract law or tort law. The major advantage for victims of misrepresentation to claim under the ordinance is that the burden of proof is shifted from the victim/claimant to the offending party. The offender is to prove that its statement was honest and made reasonably. Under the ordinance, the offending party thus has the responsibility to prove that there was no fraud or negligence in its statement.

Generally, misrepresentations fall into three categories: innocent, fraudulent, and negligent. We will now discuss these categories in turn. For the sake of completeness, we will also review the traditional remedies available to a victim of misrepresentation.

1. Innocent misrepresentation

The first type of misrepresentation to be discussed is innocent misrepresentation. *Innocent misrepresentation* occurs where one party (the offending party) makes a false statement about a material fact believing it to be true.[17] A statement is *material* if it induced the other party (the innocent party) to enter the contract. In other words, the innocent party would not have entered the contract except for that statement. Compared with the other two types of misrepresentation, an innocent misrepresentation is easier to prove because the innocent party does not have to establish the offending party's fraud or negligence in making the false statement. The innocent party will have the right to cancel the contract. As such, the innocent party can terminate the contract (known as *rescission* or *rescinding* the contract), and have any property or money returned, so long as the innocent party can return any property obtained under the contract in or near the property's original condition. This is pursuant to a principle known as *restitutio in integrum*—that is, rescission,[18] which might include indemnity for the expenses required by the contract. Thus, rescission is intended to return the parties to their pre-contractual positions.

Generally, no damages can be claimed for innocent misrepresentation.[19] The remedy of rescission may be lost in the following situations:

- The injured party states its intent to proceed with the contract after it has realised the misstatement of fact, i.e., the innocent party *affirms* the contract.
- *Restitutio in integrum* is impossible (e.g., the goods are no longer in existence).
- *Laches* (i.e., too much time) had passed before the claim was made.[20]
- The contract was fully executed. However, this common law rule has been changed by section 2 of the Misrepresentation Ordinance (Cap 284).[21]
- A *bona fide* purchaser for value[22] without notice of the dispute has intervened.

2. *Fraudulent misrepresentation*

Another category of misrepresentation involves fraud.[23] *Fraudulent misrepresentation* is where a contracting party gains an advantage:

- by lying about a material fact
- when the other contracting party relied on the lie
- which resulted in economic injury to the innocent party

The innocent party's reliance on the alleged fraudulent misrepresentation must have been reasonable in order to successfully claim fraud.

Fraud is defined as existing when a 'false representation was made (1) knowingly, or, (2) without belief in its truth, or (3) recklessly, careless of whether the representation was true or false'.[24] Fraudulent misrepresentation is *not* a dispute concerning a future promise or a future act, because this would be a claim for breach of contract. Rather, fraudulent misrepresentation must be a false representation of some present fact and not future intent.

To establish fraud, it is necessary to prove the lack of an honest belief in the truth of what was stated.[25] 'The converse of this is that however negligent a person may be, he cannot be liable for fraud, provided that his belief is honest; mere carelessness is not sufficient, although gross carelessness may justify an inference that he was not honest.'[26] Nonetheless, a mere allegation that the offending party never intended to perform a contract which the offending party made is insufficient to establish a claim for fraud.

Further, the misrepresentation must be made with the intent to defraud or mislead the innocent party. Should a third party learn of the misrepresentation and subsequently relies on the misrepresentation, the third party has no claim for loss against the fraudulent party. The reason is because the offending party had no intention or desire to defraud the third party. For example, Alan and Calvin are in a restaurant discussing the sale of Alan's 1999 automobile, which is worth HK$90,000. Alan fraudulently states to Calvin that the car is a 2009 model which is worth HK$250,000. Keith overhears this conversation and purchases the car from Alan for HK$175,000. Keith cannot claim fraudulent misrepresentation as a vitiating factor in his contract with Alan.

If fraudulent misrepresentation is proven, there is no requirement for *restitutio in integrum*. The fraudulent party must return any property of the innocent party obtained by fraud. In addition, the innocent party may claim damages from the fraudulent party. Any party induced or persuaded to enter a contract by misrepresentation concerning an essential term, upon which that party justifiably relied, may sue to cancel or avoid[27] the contract for fraud, and recover any money paid by the innocent party (i.e., reliance damages). *Reliance damages* is the difference between the actual worth or value that the innocent party received and what the innocent party paid the offending fraudulent party. Alternatively, the innocent party may recover restitution damages to the extent that the offending party profited by the misrepresentation. If the property cannot be returned to the innocent party, the amount of damages will be increased to compensate for the loss.

According to one authority, section 3(1) of the Misrepresentation Ordinance (Cap 284) provides:

> that where the representee suffers loss as a result of making a contract with the representor following the latter's misrepresentation, the representor will have to pay damages unless he can prove that he genuinely *and reasonably* believed in the truth of his statement up to the time when the contract was made. The loss-suffering representee thus does not have to prove fault on the representor's part; *the representor has to disprove it*. Given this reversal of the normal burden of proof, an action under this sub-section will almost always be preferable . . .
> . . . damages under this subsection are tortious. The purpose of tort damages is to put the claimant, as far as money can do, into his pre-tort position. Thus the representee, under section 3(1), should

> be put back to the position he would have been in had the misrepresentation not induced him to make the contract. Contractual damages, on the other hand, seek to put the claimant into the position he should have been had the contract been fulfilled.[28]

Although not discussed here as it does not pertain directly to contract law, the innocent party may also sue for economic damages in tort law by claiming and proving deceit.

3. Negligent misrepresentation

The third category of misrepresentation is negligent misrepresentation.[29] A *negligent misstatement* is a representation made carelessly to a party who is persuaded by the statement to act to its detriment.[30] When an offending party makes a false statement honestly believed to be true but the statement was made without a reasonable ground for such a belief, there is negligent misrepresentation.

Negligent misrepresentation arises usually where a professional, such as an accountant, lawyer, or architect, breaches a duty owed to the innocent party to provide accurate information. The professional is not liable to everyone, but only to those whom a duty is owed. A duty arises under the privity of contract between the innocent party and the offending party, or the equivalent of privity for those who were the 'end and aim' of the business transaction. Alternatively, an obligation arises where the recipient of the statement was within a group of persons to whom the statement was directed. There is some contact or awareness between the professional and the actual injured party.

The offending party may have failed to use reasonable care to determine the true facts or failed to apply the skill and competence of a reasonable person in the offending party's profession. As such, an offending party who negligently supplies information may be liable for the economic or financial loss suffered by the recipient of that information.

In summary, the party making the negligent misstatement will be liable for any loss suffered by the innocent party if:

- the statement was untrue;
- the statement was material, i.e., concerning matters relevant to some essential aspect or subject of pre-contractual negotiations;
- the maker of the statement owes a duty of care to the recipient of the statement, i.e., the innocent party;
- the maker of the statement did not exclude liability, or if the maker did exclude liability, the exemption clause is not reasonable;

- a reasonable person acting prudently and cautiously would not have made this statement; and
- it was reasonable for the recipient, i.e., the innocent party, to have relied on this statement.

The remedy for economic or financial loss resulting from negligent misstatement is compensation known as *damages*. (The topic of damages is discussed in Chapter 7.) Other possible remedies, depending upon the factual situation, might include bringing a case in tort (e.g., claiming negligence in making the representation), rescission of the contract, or damages under the Misrepresentation Ordinance discussed above.

The case of *Ngai Keung v Ming Yiu Heng* [2012] HKEC 1002 summarised some of the principles discussed in this section. The court stated:

> 5. The legal principles involved in this case are: rescission, misrepresentation and duress. Except for the question whether rescission is open to a representee who has the opportunity to discover the falsity of the representation, counsel have no dispute about these trite principles. For convenience, these general principles are set out hereunder.
>
> 6. In general, the equitable remedy of rescission is available to a representee who can show that a false representation was made to him by or on behalf of the other party to the contract; that either the representation was made fraudulently or it was a representation of fact; and that the representation acted as an inducement to his decision to enter into the contract: see Cartwright, *Misrepresentation, Mistake and Non-Disclosure*, Third Edition, at paragraph 4-21. Of particular relevance in this case, as the facts reveal, is that the representee must show that he has relied on the representation in the meaning that the court is satisfied is false: *Misrepresentation, Mistake and Non-Disclosure*, paragraph 5-24.
>
> 7. A misrepresentation must be a false statement of fact, past or present, as distinct from a statement of opinion, or of intention, or of law. A mere statement of opinion which proves to have been unfounded or a simple statement of intention which is not put into effect, as a general rule, cannot be regarded as a representation of fact, unless such opinion or intention is not honesty held: *Misrepresentation, Mistake and Non-Disclosure*, paragraphs 6-004 to 6-008.
>
> 8. A contract which has been entered into as the result of duress may be avoided by the party who was threatened. Threat to the victim's person as well as wrongful threats to his property may

> amount to duress: *Misrepresentation, Mistake and Non-Disclosure*, paragraph 7-001.
>
> . . .
>
> 15. . . . it is difficult to see how . . . [contributory negligence] could be raised as a defence to an action for rescission of a contract due to misrepresentation which vitiated the consent needed to make a binding agreement. If in the course of negotiating a contract, one party made a representation to the other which induced that other party to enter into a contract, it certainly lies ill in the representator's mouth to say that the representee should have verified the truth or otherwise of what he was told. To import a duty on the representee to verify the representation . . . would be to impose on the representee a due diligence duty which he has not contracted to undertake and to relieve the representor of the consequence of his own wrong while allowing him to keep the benefit of the contract. This is contrary to good commercial practice and commercial morality. It is also contrary to public policy. . . . I conclude that that a misrepresentee might have discovered the falsity of the misrepresentation is no defence to a claim for rescission.

ii. Mistake: Generally

Mistake is a difficult topic to understand. Academics have attributed this difficulty to the following:

- lacking conceptual unity[31]
- overlapping with other areas of contract law such as offer and acceptance, misrepresentation, and frustration[32]
- being the most perplexing and academically complex topic found in contract law[33]
- consuming inordinate amount of space in a textbook or class but not in real life[34]

Reading some of the academic treatises on this subject of mistake will reveal a lack of uniformity in the use of the terms associated with mistake. So, why is mistake so important? According to one source, it is because mistake is the only vitiating factor under the common law that could make the agreement void rather than voidable.[35] However, before proceeding to discuss this vitiating factor further, we first define the term *mistake* and the different types of mistake.

A mistake occurs when one party is wrong about some aspect of the proposed contract so that there is no actual agreement between the parties. In more technical language, a mistake is an erroneous belief, which is not in accordance with the facts. Mistake thus pertains to the formation of a legally binding agreement:

- Was there a lack of subject matter, that is, was there anything about which to make a contract?
- Was there a lack of agreement, that is, was there a lack of consent?

The law will provide a remedy only when the mistake is operative. An *operative* mistake pertains to the terms of the contract, and whether a reasonable person would have made such a mistake.[36] The consequence of an operative mistake is that the contract is void *ab initio* (i.e., void from the beginning).[37]

Where mistake is proven, the remedy known as *rectification* is available. Rectification is an equitable remedy available where a written agreement can be proved not to reflect the prior oral agreement.[38] A court may rewrite the contract in order to represent the parties' true intentions.[39]

The court in *Codelfa Construction Proprietary Ltd v State Rail Authority of NSW* (1982) 149 CLR 337 explained the difference between *rectification* and an *implied term* (previously discussed in Chapter 4, section B) as follows:

> In each case the problem is caused by a deficiency in the expression of the consensual agreement. A term which should have been included has been omitted. The difference is that with rectification the term which has been omitted and should have been included was actually agreed upon; with implication the term is one which it is presumed that the parties would have agreed upon had they turned their minds to it—it is not a term that they have actually agreed upon. Thus, in the case of the implied term the deficiency in the expression of the consensual agreement is caused by the failure of the parties to direct their minds to a particular eventuality and to make explicit provision for it. Rectification ensures that the contract gives effect to the parties' actual intention; the implication of a term is designed to give effect to the parties' presumed intention.[40]

Hong Kong's High Court in *Jardine Engineering Corporation Ltd v Shimizu Corporation* [1992] 2 HKC 271, 310 referred to this explanation with approval.

At law, there are three types of mistake that can vitiate a contract: unilateral, common, and mutual mistake. The reader should be aware that mistake can also be categorised as one of fact or of law.[41] However, here we consider only the first category containing the three types of mistakes.

1. Unilateral mistake

The first of these types of mistake to be reviewed is known as *unilateral mistake*, which occurs where only one party is in error. This party does not know the true state of affairs or makes an incorrect assumption in entering a contract and the other party knows or ought to know of this mistake.[42] With unilateral mistake, consent between the parties is negatived or negated as the parties do not reach an agreement.

An example of unilateral mistake over a term of the contract can be found in the Hong Kong case of *Wong Tak-sing v Amertex International* [1988] 1 HKLR 98. This case involved a $350,000 debt over which the parties' solicitors were negotiating a settlement. The plaintiff's lawyers offered in writing to accept $25,000 as settlement when the lawyers actually meant $250,000. Before any correction could be made, the defendant's solicitors accepted the offer. The court found that there was an operative unilateral mistake, i.e., 'an attempt to accept an offer which the offeree knew the offeror never intended'.[43]

Another frequently cited example of unilateral mistake concerns mistaken identity. This occurs when one party impersonates another person while negotiating in person with the innocent party. The innocent party has mistaken the identity of the pretender and enters into a contract with this impostor. The court in *Lewis v Averay* [1972] 1 QB 198 held that, under this factual scenario, the mistake was not operative and the contract was not void. A more recent English case has confirmed that in situations where the parties are negotiating face-to-face, and one party is an impostor, the innocent party's claim of unilateral mistake likely will fail. The reason is because the innocent party's offer is made to the imposter, that is, the other party who is physically present rather than to the person the imposter is impersonating. *Shogun Finance Ltd v Hudson* [2004] 1 All ER 215.

A unilateral mistake is generally no defence or excuse for the mistaken party to avoid performance of its contractual obligations. There is, generally, no requirement on the other party to correct the error of the mistaken party. Nonetheless, the other party must do nothing to mislead the mistaken party, whether actively or passively, even by silence. If the mistake is self-caused and concerns the quality or characteristics of an object, the general rule is that there will be no remedy for the mistaken party. If the mistake concerns the scope of an offer, so that the mistaken party believes that the subject matter of the contract is essentially different in kind from what it actually is, and the other party is aware of this, there is a duty on the other party to correct the mistake. If the other party does not correct the mistake, the contract will be void as there can be no acceptance of an offer not made.[44] Further, a unilateral mistake by one party as to the contract value (i.e., the price being paid) or to the extent of the labour or materials required to perform the contract is an error of business judgment, which is not generally a ground to rescind the contract.

2. *Common mistake*

Common mistake occurs when both parties make the same fundamental mistake concerning the contract. In this situation, there is a lack of the subject matter of the contract.[45] With a common mistake, the parties have come to an agreement but that agreement was based on a common or shared error about some item which was essential to the contract. Hence, a shared mistake vitiates the contract because the agreement is based on a falsehood. One frequent example of a common mistake nullifying consent is where the parties agree to the rental of a recital hall without realising that the recital hall had burned down.[46]

At common law, the contract will be void for common mistake if the mistake is sufficiently fundamental or extreme. In the case of *Great Peace Shipping Ltd v Tsavliris (International) Ltd* [2003] QB 679, the English Court of Appeal listed the requirements for a common mistake to exist:

- There must be a common assumption as to the existence of a state of affairs.
- There must be no warranty by either party that that state of affairs exists.
- The non-existence of the state of affairs must not be attributable to the fault of either party.
- The non-existence of the state of affairs must render performance of the contract impossible.
- The state of affairs may be the existence, or a vital attribute, of the consideration to be provided or the circumstance which must subsist if performance of the contractual adventure is to be possible.[47]

Whether a common mistake as to the quality, rather than the existence, of an item will render a resulting contract void is unclear. The general rule is that there will be a valid contract and no operative common mistake. For the moment, the case of *Bell v Lever Brothers* [1932] AC 161 seems to set out the rule. In this case, the court stated that a:

> mistake will not affect assent unless it is the mistake of both parties and is as to the existence of some quality which makes the thing

> without the quality essentially different from the thing as it was believed to be.[48]. . .
>
> [For example,] A buys a picture from B: both A and B believe it to be the work of an old master, and a high price is paid. It turns out to be a modern copy. A has no remedy in the absence of representation or warranty.[49]

Equity may allow the remedy of rescission in situations where the contract is not void at common law. If it is equitable to do so, the contract will be declared voidable by the court, and either or both parties may seek to avoid this contract. Note that, under equity, this contract is not void *ab initio*, i.e., void from the beginning. Thus, a court will impose whatever terms it considers to be fair before the contract may be avoided. In the *Great Peace Shipping Ltd* case, the court stated that if a contract is not void under the common law, equity will not be able to nullify this contract on the basis of common mistake. Consequently, this case from the United Kingdom has restricted the application of equity where common mistake is claimed.[50]

3. Mutual mistake

Mutual mistake occurs when the parties are at cross-purposes; there is a complete lack of agreement. Unlike common mistake, the situation with mutual mistake involves each party making a different mistake about the contract terms.[51] Consequently, there is no consent between the parties, as there is no *meeting of the minds* in that there has not been an acceptance of a corresponding offer. As one source explains, a mutual mistake can be viewed as 'a question of ineffective offer and acceptance'.[52] Like a unilateral mistake, the consent of the parties in a mutual mistake is negatived or negated. The court will decide which version is more reasonable, based upon the facts, and will uphold the contract on this basis.[53]

A brief summary of this section on the topic of *mistake* can be found in the Court of Final Appeal's recent statement on the topics of unilateral mistake, mutual mistake, and rectification in *Kowloon Development Finance Ltd v Pendex Industries Ltd* (2013) 16 HKCFAR 336. This case involved Kowloon Development as the lender and Pendex Industries as the borrower who failed to repay the loan. A dispute arose concerning the interpretation of the trial court's orders with regard to the revised re-payment schedule, particularly whether Kowloon Development could sue Pendex for the outstanding amount of the original loan. Kowloon Development claimed the trial court's order should be invalidated because of mistake and/or the trial court's order should be rectified. The lower court decided in favour of Kowloon Development for rectification based on both common and unilateral mistake. In deciding against Pendex Industries, the Court of Final Appeal stated:

> 19. . . . first I should say something about the legal requirements of mutual and unilateral mistake in an action for rectification. They sound like two varieties of mistake about the same thing, made in the one case by both parties and in the other by only one of them. But they are actually the expression of quite different principles. They deal with different kinds of mistakes. In the case of mutual or common mistake—the adjectives are in this context interchangeable—the mistake is about whether a written document correctly reflects what the parties had, on an objective assessment, agreed it should contain. As Denning LJ said in the well-known case of *Frederick E Rose (London) Ltd v William H Pim Jnr & Co Ltd* [1953] 2 QB 450, 461: "Rectification [for mutual mistake] is concerned with contracts and documents, not with intentions". . . . the concept of rectification for common mistake involves carrying into effect what the parties appear to have actually agreed that the document should say. And in deciding what the parties have agreed, the common law adopts its usual objective stance, looking at what a reasonable observer would have understood the parties to mean and not concerning itself with their uncommunicated states of mind . . .
>
> 20. Rectification for unilateral mistake, on the other hand, is very much concerned with the subjective states of mind of the parties. If the contract contains a provision which one party knows that the other party thinks is not there, or knows that the other party is mistaken about its meaning, the court may, as a matter of discretion, either refuse to allow him to enforce the contract as it would ordinarily be construed . . . or go further and rectify the written agreement to give effect to what the mistaken party thought had been agreed . . .
>
> 21. The difference between the two grounds for rectification may be illustrated by the facts of *Rose v Pim*. The plaintiff was a London merchant who placed a written order for Moroccan horsebeans in the belief that his Egyptian buyer would accept them under the description "feveroles". He had discussed this with the seller, another London merchant who was of the same opinion. But the parties were mistaken. In Egypt, horsebeans and feveroles are different. The Court of Appeal refused to rectify the order by substituting "feveroles" for "horsebeans" because the document did not differ from what, to all outward appearances, the parties had agreed. They had agreed on a sale of horsebeans and the order document said "horsebeans". On the other hand, if the seller knew that the buyer

> mistakenly thought that it was a term of the contract that horse-beans could be sold as feveroles, a court might have thought he had contracted in bad faith and that the order should be rectified on the ground of unilateral mistake.
>
> . . .
>
> 23. . . . The function of the court is to make the document accord with what the parties objectively agreed. . . . the important difference between mutual and unilateral mistake lies in what the mistake must be about. In mutual mistake, the mistake is about whether the document correctly reflects the terms previously agreed. In unilateral mistake, it is about the mistaken belief of one of the parties, known to the other, about what the contract said or meant.
>
> 24. Before leaving this discussion of general principles, I should emphasise that in claims for rectification of contracts for mutual mistake, it is necessary for the court to be confident that the formal document does not reflect what was previously agreed. As Denning LJ said in *Rose v Pim*, 461, "if you can predicate with certainty what their contract was, and that it is, by common mistake, wrongly expressed in the document, then you rectify the document; but nothing less will suffice."[54]

4. Non est factum

The defence of *non est factum*[55] is available where the signer is an innocent victim of fraud or misrepresentation such that there is a radical difference between what was actually signed and what was thought to have been signed. The contract was signed by error, without knowledge of the agreement's meaning. However, this defence is not available to a signer who was negligent or careless in signing, e.g., who did not read the document or signed it in blank, according to the court in *Saunders v Anglia Building Society* [1971] AC 1004. The court stated that there

> must I think be a radical difference between what he signed and what he thought he was signing—or one could use the words 'fundamental' or 'serious' or 'very substantial'.[56]

Several Hong Kong cases have considered the claim of *non est factum*. In *Lee Tit Fan v Strong Base International Industrial Ltd* [2012] HKEC 512, the court summarised the legal principles applying to *non est factum*:

> (1) The burden of proving fraud and establishing non nest [*sic*] factum is on the party who seeks to invoke this remedy and the burden is a heavy one . . .

> (2) The standard of proof should [be] commensurate with the seriousness of the nature of the alleged misconduct, i.e., the more serious the allegation, the less likely it is that the event occurred and hence, the stronger should be in the evidence before the court concludes that the allegation is established on the balance of probability: *Nina Kung v Wang Din Shin [2005] 8 HKCFAR 387 at 440.*
>
> (3) The court will entertain a plea on non est factum if satisfied that "consent was truly lacking" but will require of signers to act responsibly and carefully according to their circumstances in putting their signature to the document.[57]

Likewise, in the case of *Pathak Ravi Dutt v Sanjeev Maheshwari* [2014] 3 HKLRD 597, the court stated:

> 20. The basis of the plaintiff's case is that although he signed the . . . Contract, he did not know that it was a contract for his employment as a domestic helper of the defendant in Hong Kong, as he did not know English and could neither read nor understand the . . . Contract, and the defendant had not explained it to him. The defendant merely produced the document and asked him to sign, and he did so on the basis of his trust of the defendant.
>
> 21. It is trite that it is no answer for a person to disclaim a contract on the basis only that he did not know or read what he was signing. A lack of understanding of the contents, meaning, terms or effect of a document signed by a person of full age and understanding is not a ground to disown the document. In *Bank of China (Hong Kong) Ltd v Fung Chin Kan* (2002) 5 HKCFAR 515 at 533, Litton NPJ stated the following fundamental principle:
>
>> generally speaking, when a person signs a legal document, he or she is bound by the act of signature: As a matter of general law, it is no defence to say that he or she did not understand the contents of a legal document; that person takes the chance of being bound by its terms, as he or she can take the simple precaution of not signing until its contents have been fully explained and understood.
>
> 22. As Ribeiro PJ also explained in his judgment in *Ming Shiu Chung v Ming Shiu Sum* (2006) 9 HKCFAR 334, at 361:
>
>> Reliance is universally placed on signatures appended to documents by persons of full age and understanding as signifying the signatory's assent or adherence to what that document states. Wheresuch a person has signed a document which purports to have legal

> effect, the law has never regarded it as enough to show that he signed without knowing its contents for the document to be disavowed. It is an everyday occurrence that people sign documents without reading the small (or even the large) print and therefore signed without actually knowing the terms (or all the terms) of the documents signed. But they are held to be documents which they have chosen to sign unless there is shown to be recognised legal basis for concluding that their apparent consent has been in some way vitiated or that reliance on the document by some other person falls into some category of unconscionable conduct justifying relief in equity.[58]

As can be seen from the above cases, claiming *non est factum* as a defence is difficult to establish, as no negligence by the signatory is allowed. Yet, if the *non est factum* defence succeeds, the contract is void *ab initio* (from the beginning). This defence is available for cases of mistake, duress, and undue influence.

iii. Duress

A contract is voidable if a party signs a contract involuntarily out of fear, which has been created by the following:

- a threat of violence
- actual violence
- threat of arrest
- false imprisonment
- wrongful prosecution
- blackmail
- a threat to take goods
- the actual seizure of the goods

The party must have no alternative but to agree to enter the contract or to its modification. The party's consent to the contract is not voluntarily given but is unfairly coerced so that free will has been overcome. Simply put, the party was forced or pressured to sign the contract against its wish.[59]

In order to be a vitiating factor, the duress must be one reason, although it need not be the only reason, to agree to the contract. Further, the coercion must be unlawful. For example, Alan has a legitimate right to file a lawsuit against Kevin. There is no duress by Alan threatening a lawsuit if Kevin does not sign the written agreement. Note that the victim of the violence or the subject of the threat may be someone other than the contracting party, e.g., a relative or friend.[60]

In 1976, courts recognised economic duress[61] to be an operative factor.[62] Economic duress occurs where a party is coerced into an unfavourable renegotiation of the contract. In these cases, consideration has been provided for the change, but that change has been against the will of a party.[63] Economic duress makes a contract voidable, but not void. The factors in deciding whether there is duress are the existence of alternatives and the extent to which those alternatives have been considered.[64]

The Court of Appeal has set out Hong Kong's position on the illegitimate use of power in economic duress cases. In *Esquire (Electronics) Ltd v Hong Kong and Shanghai Banking Corp Ltd* [2007] 3 HKLRD 439, the court stated:

> 153. The reason that the law enables the weaker party to avoid a contract entered into under duress is that
>
> > . . . his apparent consent was induced by pressure exercised upon him by that other party which the law does not regard as legitimate, with the consequence that the consent is treated in law as revocable unless approbated either expressly or by implication after the illegitimate pressure has ceased to operate on his mind. It is a rationale similar to that which underlies the avoidability of contracts entered into and the recovery of money exacted under colour of office, or under undue influence or in consequence of threats of physical duress.
>
> *per* Lord Diplock in *Universe Tankships Inc of Monrovia v International Transport Workers Federation & Others* [1983] 1 AC 366 at p. 384.
>
> 154. The key to proving economic duress is proof of the illegitimacy of the suggested pressure. Much commercial activity necessarily involves pressure, often considerable and sometimes overwhelming, exercised by parties who find themselves in powerful bargaining positions. But that of itself is not illegitimate.[65]

Pao On v Lau Yiu Long [1980] AC 614 (PC) remains a leading case on economic duress. Company A agreed to sell shares to Company B. Under the main agreement, Company B had to keep the shares for a certain time. To safeguard against a fall in the shares' value, there was a subsidiary agreement where Company A was to buy back 60 per cent of the shares at a set price. Company B, concerned over a loss in profits if the share price rose, refused to continue with the main agreement unless Company A cancelled the subsidiary agreement and agreed to an indemnity clause if the share price fell. Company A refused to honour the indemnity clause when the share price fell, claiming that the indemnity clause was the result of duress. The court determined that there had been no duress because there had to be coercion of will, rather than a change in circumstance, in order to vitiate consent.

A coerced transaction may, nonetheless, be accepted after the coercion or pressure has ended. In other words, the coerced party may ratify the contract. The ratification may recognise the validity of the contract. The ratification may also prevent any claims for a remedy or for damages, if the party does not promptly move to have a court rescind the contract once the pressure is removed.

iv. Undue Influence

As discussed above, duress involves coercion. Undue influence involves something less than coercion. As noted by one court:

> At common law, duress was justified on the ground that the duress prevented the affected party from forming a full and independent resolution to the contract. The doctrine of undue influence has wider application . . . It ensures that no person should be allowed to retain the benefit of his own fraud or wrongful act.[66]

Undue influence involves unfair persuasion by the stronger party. The stronger party abuses its position of trust and confidence or uses psychological dominance to obtain an advantage or profit at the expense of the susceptible and weaker party.[67] Undue influence allows a weaker party to avoid a contract on the basis that the weaker party's consent was not voluntary. The contract is thus voidable at the choice of the party under undue influence. Undue influence is an equitable doctrine,[68] which may allow the innocent party access to equitable relief, including rescission.[69]

Undue influence is usually found in situations where a weaker party places trust and confidence in the stronger party. Traditionally, undue influence is presumed between parties of certain special relationships.[70] These special relationships overlap with, but are not the same as, fiduciary relationships.[71] For example, the presumption is applied between a spiritual adviser and advised, a doctor and patient (who do not have a fiduciary relationship), but not between an agent and principal (who do have a fiduciary relationship). The court said in *Royal Bank of Scotland v Etridge (No. 2)* [2001] 4 All ER 449 that the presumption in these situations is that one party placed trust and confidence in the other, but not that the confidence is abused. However, in certain circumstances, e.g., where the transaction is clearly disadvantageous to the weaker party, undue influence may be inferred. The stronger party may counter this inference by showing that the weaker party had obtained independent advice.

Undue influence may also be applied by a third party over a party to the contract.[72] For example, a husband may unduly influence his wife to enter into guarantee contracts with a bank in order to secure his own debts. In such a case, the contract is voidable if the opposite party (the bank) has actual knowledge or suspicion that the other party (the wife) entered into the contract under undue influence from a third party (the husband). In *Royal Bank of Scotland*, the court concluded that a bank should be suspicious if a wife offers to guarantee payment of her husband's debt, as it is not to the wife's financial benefit and there is substantial risk that the husband has exerted undue influence. The bank has to take reasonable steps to ensure that the possible consequences of the transaction are made clear to the wife, e.g., by ensuring that the wife has received independent legal advice. If the bank fails to do so and the husband has exercised undue influence, the bank will be considered to have knowledge of undue influence being used against the wife.[73]

In *Diners Club International v Ng Chi-sing*, unreported, (1986) CA 143/85, affirmed on appeal [1986] HKEC 113 (CA), the trial court found that the credit card company had exercised improper pressure on Mr. Ng to guarantee payment of credit card debts of over HK$1,100,000 incurred by his son and his son's friend, by threatening to report the case to the police. As a result, the guarantee was voidable. The trial court decided that:

> Ng Yan Kiang, a man of 60 and hard of hearing, was confronted at about 7 pm [in his home] by three men who were determined to persuade him to sign the guarantees. . . . The three men did not leave until about 11 pm when they had achieved their object.
> . . . [Ng Yan Kiang] had been about to go out, with his wife, at the invitation of two relatives who were at his home. Because the uninvited and unexpected callers insisted on discussing their business, he was obliged to send his relatives ahead of him to a restaurant, from which during the remainder of the evening these relatives continually telephoned him to find out when he would join them.
>
> Ng Yan Kiang told his callers that he wanted to discuss the matter with his son before he signed but they would not allow him to do so. He had no opportunity to take independent advice, to consult his son or to think matters over and did not understand

> the full significance of what he was being asked to do. His visitors deliberately aroused anxiety in him (he called it fear) by suggesting that his son might be reported to the Commercial Crimes Bureau . . . with possible disastrous consequences for the son. . . .
>
> They deliberately sought to misrepresent the extent of the guarantees sought, implying that they would be of only temporary effect. They also deliberately attempted to mislead him as to the size of the financial commitment he was being asked to undertake.
>
> [He] was unwilling to sign, the two or three hours spent in overcoming his resistance testify to that. . . . Finally, under the pressure exerted upon him, his resistance collapsed. As he put it, he felt he had no choice. . . . [T]he signing of the forms could not be described as being based upon the free and voluntary agency of the individual.[74]

Kwok Wing Kiu v Boxing Promotions Ltd [2013] HKEC 798 is a more recent case concerning vitiating factors, in particular undue influence. The court stated:

> 31. However, as to whether the plaintiff can avail herself of the "presumption of undue influence", it is important to take heed of the judgment of the Court of Final Appeal in *Li Sau Ying v Bank of China (Hong Kong) Ltd* (2004) 7 HKCFAR 579 , which is the leading local case authority on undue influence. In that case, Lord Scott of Foscote NPJ, who gave the judgment of the Court of Final Appeal, said,
>
>> 30. The strong message from *Royal Bank of Scotland Plc v Etridge (No 2)* [2001] UKHL 44 therefore is that, particularly in Class 2B cases, concentration on a so-called presumption of undue influence is likely to detract from the real issue, namely, whether the evidence justifies a conclusion that the impugned transaction was procured by undue influence.
>>
>> . . .
>>
>> 34. I do not wish to leave this issue without expressing the hope that in future cases, where undue influence has to be proved but where the relationship between the parties is not a relationship that falls within Slade LJ's Class 2A category, the parties will concentrate on whether the evidence justifies the inference that, on a balance of probabilities, the impugned transaction was procured by undue influence, that is to say, by an abuse by the allegedly dominant party of the trust and confidence reposed in him by the allegedly subservient party.

> References in such cases to, and attempts to invoke the assistance of, an alleged evidential presumption of undue influence are, in my opinion, likely to be, as they have been in this case, a source of confusion and an impediment to the evaluation of the available evidence. (emphasis supplied)

v. Unconscionable Bargain

This is a vague theory in that there is no universally accepted definition of the concept of unconscionable bargain.[75] This legal concept provides that equity will invalidate an agreement where a weaker party is victimised by a stronger party in circumstances that do not amount to duress or undue influence. The theoretical doctrine of unconscionable bargain appears to be limited:

- Firstly, the overall bargain must be oppressive to the weaker party.
- Secondly, the doctrine may only apply when the complaining party was suffering from certain types of bargaining weakness.
- Thirdly, the stronger party must have acted unconscionably by having knowingly taken advantage of the weaker party.[76]

One source has summarised this topic thus:

> The typical indicia of an unconscionable bargain are that (1) the exploitee suffers from a serious disadvantage such as poverty or ignorance, or lack of independent advice; (2) that the exploitee has given away valuable assets or rights at a considerable undervalue, such that the terms of the bargain are oppressive; and (3) morally culpable conduct by the exploiter. Where those requirements are satisfied the onus is on the purchaser to show that the purchase was fair, just and reasonable.[77]

The case of *LZX and WYL* [2012] 5 HKLRD 29 concerned the heirs of an estate. The second wife of the deceased is from the Mainland and relatively uneducated. One of the sisters of the deceased was the executrix of the estate. The executrix was a senior government officer and auxiliary constable who had consulted a friend with legal knowledge. The second wife sought to claim her entitlement under the Inheritance (Provision for Family and Dependents) Ordinance (Cap 481). The executrix offered a payment of $50,000, allegedly threatening that the second wife would receive nothing from the estate and that she would not be allowed to return to the property where she lived.

The court referred to several cases from Hong Kong and the UK concerning unconscionable contracts. The court summarised the decisions in these cases: 'An unconscionable bargain in this context would be a bargain of an improvident character made by a poor or ignorant person acting without independent advice which cannot be shown to be a fair and reasonable transaction.'[78] Considering all the circumstances, the court concluded the parties' agreement to be unfair, unjust and unreasonable, and thus unconscionable.

The court in *Tong Kwok Cheong and Tong Wai Lin* [2014] 1 HKLRD 339 (CA) also addressed the behaviour of the stronger party in terms of deciding which party bears the burden of proof. The Court of Appeal mentioned the following points:

- One party has imposed the objectionable terms in a morally reprehensible manner.
- The term *unconscionable* relates to the behaviour of the stronger party characterised by moral culpability or impropriety.
- There has been unconscientious or extortionate abuse of power by the stronger party.
- The plaintiff is to prove unconscionable conduct, i.e., unconscientious advantage has been taken of the plaintiff.
- In short, there needs to be misbehaviour by the stronger party that affects the conscience.[79]

A final example of an unconscionable contract is the case of *Lo Wo v Cheung Chan Ka, Joseph and Bond Star Development Ltd* [2001] 3 HKC 70. The court determined that the plaintiffs, three elderly sisters (the youngest was approximately 78 years old), were simple peasants living in a remote part of Guangdong Province. These three sisters were the heirs of a one-half interest in a North Point flat owned by their deceased sister. The defendants were involved in buying all the flats (including the subject flat) in the building for redevelopment. The defendants approached the sisters offering them HK$870,000 on the basis that more could not be paid for the property as it would be used for storing sand. The sisters entered into the sales contract by each making an 'X' on the agreement. The defendants failed to inform the sisters that other comparable flat owners received HK$2.4 million and HK$300,000 removal expenses. The court decided this contract to be unconscionable for many reasons including the following:

1. Ensuring that the sisters entered into the contract quickly without adequate time for considering the proposal

2. Deliberately not informing the sisters as to the purchase prices of the other flats in the building
3. Defendant Cheung lying to the sisters that the flat was to be acquired by the developer to store sand rather than for property redevelopment
4. Dangling the HK$50,000 cash deposit before the sisters, knowing that to the rural plaintiffs and their relatives this was a large sum
5. By offering to serve as the sisters' attorney and the administrator of their deceased sister's estate, thereby depriving the sisters of proper legal representation and independent advice, and minimising the risk of the sisters withdrawing from the agreement
6. By deliberately not informing the sisters that they should have independent professional advice to review the transaction and not giving the sisters time to seek such advice
7. By not explaining to the sisters that the transaction was extraordinarily disadvantageous to the plaintiffs and that they did not seem to be capable of making judgment of what was in their best interests
8. By not giving a copy of the contract to the sisters

Note the effects of two ordinances upon this area of contract law, namely, the Supply of Services (Implied Terms) Ordinance (Cap 457) and the Unconscionable Contracts Ordinance (Cap 458).[80]

vi. Illegal and Void Contracts

In this section, we examine some situations where an agreement contains all the required elements to be a contract but yet is not legally enforceable as a contract. Generally, the reasons for non-enforcement of these agreements have to do with government policy.

On this subject, one authority has noted:

> There are several classes of contracts which, though perfect as to form, agreement and consideration, are not given full effect because they offend against the policy of the law. Some contracts may be illegal in the sense that they involve the commission of a legal wrong . . . or because they offend against fundamental principles of order or morality. Less objectionable contracts may be simply void by common law or statute.
>
> In respect of certain contracts invalidated under the above principles it is not absolutely clear whether they are illegal or void; but the distinction must be made, because there are differences between illegal and void contracts in respect of related agreements, severability and recovery of property transferred or money paid under such contracts.[81]

If a contract is illegal when formed, the whole purpose of the contract is illegal and the consideration is illegal. Courts will not enforce the contract or provide any remedy. The contract is void; it cannot be enforced by either party.[82] An example of an illegal contract is where the parties to a construction contract agree to bypass the required approval from the Building Authority.[83]

Two recent court cases involved illegal contracts and public policy. (Public policy is discussed below.) Both cases concerned agreements to develop houses on lands under the Small House Policy in the New Territories of Hong Kong. In order to build a *ting uk* under the Small House Policy, an applicant was required to certify his status as an indigenous villager. In each of these two cases, the court found that there was fraudulent misrepresentation by the applicant and refused to order enforcement of the agreement on public policy grounds.

In the first of these two cases, *Chan Yau v Chan Calvin* [2014] 5 HKLRD 304, the court stated:

> 60. The common law on the effect of illegality on contracts is a large and evolving subject.[84]
>
> . . .
>
> 65. . . . permission to build a small house was to be granted by the Government on the basis that an applicant was both the legal and beneficial owner of the land in question, the villager's application would involve a misrepresentation to the Government that he was the legal and beneficial owner of the land . . . the misrepresentation was made with knowledge that it was false . . . the contract would be illegal under common law and it would be against public policy for the Court to lend its aid to its performance. . . . the decision has been followed as authority for the proposition that a contract for small house development that necessarily involves a fraudulent misrepresentation to the Government with regard to the beneficial ownership of land is unenforceable in the courts: see e.g. *Chung Mui Teck* [2001] 2 HKLRD 471; *Lau Ting Tai v Chung Chun Kwong* [2010] 3 HKC 352; *Tang Teng Hong Tso v Cheung Tin Wah* [2014] 2 HKLRD 1032.[85]

Likewise, in the second case, *Tang Teng Hong Tso v Cheung Tin Wah* [2014] 2 HKLRD 1032, the court followed precedent and stated:

> 21. The principles distilled from the authorities are as follows:
>
> (1) Where an agreement is entered into for an illegal purpose, the court will not enforce it. *Best Sheen Development Ltd v Official Receiver* [2001]

1 HKLRD 866 . . . *Cheerbond Development Ltd v Tung Kwok Yu* [2010] 2 HKLRD 546.

(2) A development scheme that takes advantage of the Small House Policy under which an applicant *ting* would have to represent himself as the legal and beneficial owner of a piece of land . . . is illegal, as it would necessarily involve making of a false declaration and hence commission of the tort of misrepresentation to the Government. See *Best Sheen* . . . affirmed in *Chung Mui Teck v Hang Tak Buddhist Hall Association Ltd* [2001] 2 HKLRD 471.

(3) It is no answer that no false statutory declaration has yet been made if the implementation of the scheme necessarily involves the making of such a declaration.[86]

Another example of illegality involves the interest charged on a loan. If the rate of interest charged exceeds the legal rate, the loan is considered to be usurious. This makes the loan void and unenforceable, resulting in the lender forfeiting the right to recover both the principal amount borrowed and the interest. Section 25(3) of the Money Lenders Ordinance (Cap 163) provides that a transaction shall be presumed to be extortionate if the effective rate of interest on a loan exceeds 48 per cent per annum. Such a transaction will be voided by a court only if the surrounding circumstances are considered unfair or unreasonable. Under section 24(1) of the Money Lenders Ordinance, 'any person . . . who lends money . . . at an effective rate of interest which exceeds 60[%] per annum commits an offence.' Nonetheless, it is not deemed usurious if *excessive* interest is charged after the loan or debt becomes past due because the law allows borrowers to avoid the excess interest by making timely payments under the loan contract.

A contract may be legally formed but may become illegal when performed, e.g., a contractor breaches the Building Regulations while carrying out the agreement. The contract is not necessarily void if the work to be done is not essential to the contract as a whole. A client may be able to receive compensation for loss or damage as the contractor has agreed to comply with the Building Regulations. By contrast, as discussed in Chapter 6, section D, if the contract becomes illegal due to changes in law after the contract was formed, performance is not required and is considered to be made impossible.

A contract may be found by the courts to be invalid and unenforceable under *public policy*.[87] An agreement which tends to be harmful to the public or against the public good would be invalidated on public policy grounds.[88] 'The enforcement of contractual claims is in certain circumstances against public policy. The effects of public policy differ considerably depending upon the circumstances'. [89] The doctrine of public policy is 'open-textured and flexible'[90] as well as not being fixed.[91] Hence, the exact definition and application of the public policy doctrine is vague and subject to change. However, one authority has attempted to define public policy by delineating its scope:

> Objects which on grounds of public policy invalidate contracts may, for convenience, be generally classified into five groups: first, objects which are illegal by common law or by legislation; secondly, objects injurious to good government . . . thirdly, objects which interfere with the proper working of the machinery of justice; fourthly, objects injurious to marriage and morality; and, fifthly, objects economically against the public interest.[92]

The case of *Best Sheen Development Ltd v Official Receiver* [2001] 1 HKLRD 866 is yet another case involving *ting uk* rights in the New Territories. The court stated, 'the concessionary terms in the building licence would be obtained only by a misrepresentation to Government that the Bankrupt was the legal and beneficial owner of the Land'.[93] The court also noted that a 'contract to commit a civil wrong is illegal under common law'.[94] In other words, to enforce an illegal contract would be against public policy.

When a contract contains both lawful and unlawful objectives, the illegal part may be severed (i.e., removed, deleted, or cut out) by a court. If the legal part has already been performed, then payment for that performance can be enforced in a claim for restitution. As the *Tang Teng Hong Tso* court noted:

> (4) However, a party to an illegality can recover by virtue of a legal or equitable property interest if he did not need to rely on the illegal contract for any purpose other than providing the basis of his claim to the property right.[95]

The court in *Ryder Industries Ltd v Chan Shui Woo* [2014] HKEC 1566 provided a summary of these principles:

- Illegality is an aspect of public policy.
- Courts generally will not enforce a contract which is illegal either under local law or the law at the place where the contract is to be performed.
- Courts generally will enforce the portions of the contract which are not illegal.

The court stated that it is a 'well-established principle that if a claimant seeking to enforce a contract does not need to rely on his illegal performance then the contract is enforceable'.[96]

6
Discharge of Contract

Discharge of a contract refers to ending the contractual obligations between the parties. A contract ends when no further rights or obligations remain under the agreement. As stated by one authority:

> The ways in which a contractual promise may be discharged may be classified under two basic headings: discharge in accordance with the contract and discharge 'against' the contract.
>
> The former covers (1) discharge by performance and (2) discharge as a result of an event stipulated in the contract. The latter covers (a) discharge by rescission for such matters as breach or misrepresentation or by subsequent agreement; (b) discharge by frustration; and (c) discharge as a result of certain miscellaneous events such as merger and (in some cases) death or bankruptcy.[1]

We will now review each of these in turn.

A. Performance

A contract ends when the parties have done that which they promised to do under their contract. In other words, the contract is completed as the parties have performed all that they are obligated to do under the agreement. The general rule, though, is that both parties must do precisely what they promised to do before there can be discharge of a contract by performance.[2] There are some exceptions to this general rule and the applicability of these exceptions may depend upon whether the contract is *entire* or *divisible*:

> A contract is said to be "entire" when complete performance by one party is a condition precedent to the liability of the other; in such a

> contract the consideration is usually a lump sum which is payable only upon complete performance by the other party (hence, the reference is sometimes to a "lump sum contract"). The opposite of an "entire contract" is a "divisible contract", which is separable into parts, so that different parts of the consideration may be assigned to severable parts of the performance, e.g. an agreement for payment pro rata.[3]

Refer to the scenario in Chapter 4 involving Alice and her purchase of a black Sub-Zero® refrigerator for her new home on the Peak. This scenario can be considered as an example of a lump sum contract involving the sale and delivery of the black Sub-Zero® refrigerator to Alice. Once the ordered item has been safely delivered, the shop has completely performed all its obligations under this contract, i.e., the shop's entire contract with Alice. She is now obligated to pay the full amount, the lump sum. Divisible contracts are discussed in subsection ii below.

i. Substantial Performance

Here, we discuss one exception to the rule that 'a party to a contract must perform exactly what he undertook to do'. This exception is where substantial performance of the contractual obligations has taken place.[4] *Substantial performance* means one party has substantially performed or substantially completed an entire contract but has not completed full performance.[5] In other words, if a party has substantially performed, there is no breach of condition. This doctrine of substantial performance is intended to prevent unfairness where a contract is breached unintentionally and minor non-essential deficiencies are caused, which can be easily and inexpensively remedied. The doctrine is frequently raised in disputes over construction contracts. However, it is not available for wilful or intentional breaches.

Let us return to the example concerning the black Sub-Zero® refrigerator ordered by Alice for her designer kitchen. What are the consequences if the shop delivers a yellow and purple coloured model? What are the consequences if the shop delivers a black Samsung® refrigerator? What are the consequences if the shop delivers a black Sub-Zero® refrigerator that has a scratch on the side which will be hidden once the refrigerator is installed in the cabinetry? What are the consequences if the shop delivers a black Sub-Zero® refrigerator that has a crease on the front? Has the shop made substantial performance or has the shop committed a breach of condition?

If the difference is small between the obligation as performed and the actual contracted obligation, this breach would be considered as a minor breach of the contract. The party committing this minor breach may be allowed the price agreed under the contract less a deduction for the defective performance. In other words, there will be an allowance for difference between its substantial performance and the original performance under the contract.[6]

Thus, the difference between substantial performance of the contract and complete performance of the contract is considered to be a breach of warranty. Damages for this breach of warranty will be the value of the difference between what was bargained for and what was actually received. Breach with substantial performance results in damages, usually a reduction in price. Breach of a condition results in the innocent party having the option to repudiate the contract and to sue for damages.[7]

ii. Severable Contracts

Another exception to the general rule of performance involves divisible or severable contracts. A *divisible* or *severable* contract is one in which separate 'parts' are to be delivered or performed, and separately paid. Each instalment is considered to be independent of the others, and is separately enforceable regardless of performance or non-performance of the other instalments. The performing party does not have to prove substantial performance of the entire contract to recover for the performance of one instalment.

Should a court consider a contract to be severable, the party who fails to perform all the promises can recover a portion of the contract price for performing part of the contract. Even a wilfully defaulting party is permitted a partial recovery for previously performed instalments of the severable contract. In other words, each instalment is breached one at a time unless the breach of one instalment shows an intention to repudiate the entire contract, or where the breached instalment substantially affects the value of the whole contract. Consequently, even if the performance of the first instalment was defective, the innocent party is not allowed to end the contract as long as the defaulting party has an opportunity to make good the defects in later instalments.

There is a presumption against the existence of a divisible contract. Consequently, a party seeking to separate the individual terms of the contract must prove that both parties intended a severable contract at the time of creating the contract. For example, a party may produce evidence that the parties intended instalment payments be made as work progressed in a building contract, as is the norm.[8]

iii. Part Performance

There is another exception to the general rule that a party must perform fully its contractual undertaking. This exception involves partial performance of the contract. It will be recalled that:

> Where a party has performed only part of an entire obligation it can normally recover nothing, neither the agreed price, since it is not due under the terms of the contract, nor any smaller sum for the value of its partial performance, since the court has no power to apportion the consideration. The refusal of pro rata payment is based on the inability of the court . . . to add such a provision to the contract, and also upon the rule that . . . part performance under an express contract cannot . . . justify the imposition of a restitutionary obligation to pay on a quantum meruit basis.[9]

If the innocent party had the choice of refusing part performance but accepts part performance, there is a variation in the contract.[10] Partial performance does not need to be accepted or paid for unless the contract so allows. If partial performance is accepted, it must be paid for on a *pro rata* basis.

> [A] claim may be made by a party who has not completely performed if it can be inferred from the circumstances that there is a fresh agreement between the parties that payment will be made pro rata for work already done or goods already supplied under the original contract, as for example where a buyer of goods accepts less than the stipulated quantity. It is not, however, enough to bring this principle into play that the party from whom payment is demanded has received a benefit from the partial performance; he must have had, at the time when it became clear that there would not be exact performance, an opportunity to accept or reject the partial performance. Nor is it possible where that party had no such choice to bring an action upon a quantum meruit.[11]

iv. Induced Non-performance

Another exception to the general rule of complete performance is found where one party prevents performance of the contract by the other party. In this event, the innocent party may sue for the damages resulting from this breach of contract, repudiate the contract, or both.[12] Again referring to the scenario with Alice and the black Sub-Zero® refrigerator, consider the following. The shop delivers the correct model and colour of Sub-Zero® refrigerator to Alice's new home at the specified time. Alice refuses to accept delivery. She refuses to allow the deliverymen to enter her home and orders them to leave her property. As the parties' contract provides that the shop must deliver to Alice a particular refrigerator by a particular time, Alice has prevented the shop from performing its contractual obligations. The shop can sue Alice and/or cancel the contract.

B. Agreement, Assignment, and Novation

A contract can be changed (the technical term is *varied*) or discharged by oral or written agreement.[13] A contract can be varied or discharged orally even if that contract was entered into in writing or by deed.[14] If the varying or discharging agreement is made by deed, there is no need to show consideration. A contract required to be in writing may be discharged orally, but cannot be varied unless evidenced by another contract in writing.[15]

Contractual rights, including options, may be transferred to a third party who was not named in the original contract through an *assignment*, even without the consent of the promisor.[16] However, liabilities under a contract and offers cannot be transferred without consent of the other party.[17] A contract right that has been assigned cannot be reversed if consideration has been paid for the assignment. The assignment ends the right of the party making the assignment (also referred to as the *assignor*). To revoke an assigned right, a court order for rescission is required.

Gratuitous assignments, similar to a promise to make a gift, in general can be freely revoked by the assignor. 'Assignment by act of the parties may be an assignment either of rights or of liabilities under a contract; or, as it is sometimes expressed, an assignment of the benefit or the burden of the contract.'[18]

An assignment of contract rights may arise as a guarantee for a loan, a gift, or a sale (in return for payment of the transfer of right). For example, consider a sale of a debt by the creditor to a third party, more specifically, a bank selling a long-term mortgage to another company. Additionally, as an aside, after the bank has assigned it rights to this mortgage, in order to end the assignor's right to payment under the assigned mortgage, the party receiving the assignment (also known as the *assignee*) should immediately notify the debtor. This would prevent the assignor from collecting payments from the debtor. Finally, note that an assignment may also be made through the operation of law, for example, in the event of death or bankruptcy.[19]

Novation is where a new contract is formed and substituted for the existing contract which is discharged.[20] Novation, unlike an assignment, is with the consent or agreement of all the parties to the contract.[21] It is generally the use of novation to allow the introduction of a new party to the new contract and the discharge of a party to the former contract.[22] Under the common law, novation was the only method of assigning a contractual right.[23]

C. Repudiation and Anticipatory Breach

Repudiation is the refusal by one of the contracting parties to be bound by the contract's terms.[24] When a party repudiates a contract, that party intends no longer to be under any obligations created by the contract. Repudiation may take place when performance is due.

> Instead of merely failing to provide due performance at the stipulated time, a party may put himself in breach by evincing an intention, by words or conduct, of repudiating his obligations under the contract.[25]

Repudiation may thus also take place before performance is due. This is known as *anticipatory breach* or *anticipatory repudiation*. The meaning of these two terms is that the innocent party is expecting or anticipating the other party will breach the contract before the deadline for performing the obligation or obligations. For example, refer to the scenario concerning Alice's purchase of the refrigerator. After entering the contract but before delivery of the refrigerator, Alice calls the shop. She informs the shop that she will not pay more than 75 per cent of the agreed price of the refrigerator. The shop may anticipate that Alice will breach the contract when the refrigerator is delivered and payment becomes due.

Thus, repudiation by one party amounts to the wrongful refusal by that party to fulfil its contractual obligations. This act of repudiation would allow the innocent party to consider itself discharged from its obligations and sue for breach.[26] Note that a party's request to renegotiate the contract or purchase price is not an anticipatory breach.

As explained by one source:

> Repudiation takes place where a party expressly or impliedly refuses to carry out duties under the contract. Parties may also make it impossible for themselves to carry out the contract. . . . This is a kind of repudiation.
>
> . . . The repudiation may take place before the time when performance is due. In such a case, the breach which repudiates the contract is called 'anticipatory breach'. Because a party cannot bring a

> contract to an end by breaking it, however fundamental the breach, unless the other party accepts that breach as repudiation, the injured party has a choice. When a breach is committed before the contract date of performance, it may be sufficiently serious to allow the injured party to treat it as repudiation. If it is bad enough to be treated as repudiation, the injured party may either treat the contract at once as discharged and sue for damages (and possibly some other remedy), or leave the contract in existence until the contract date for performance. If the injured party chooses to wait, the party in breach may carry out its part of the contract at any time until the contract date or the other's acceptance of the repudiation. . . .
>
> If the term broken is a warranty, the breach is not a repudiation. Of course, a complete failure to perform, such as delivering a bicycle when the contract calls for a car – sometimes called fundamental breach – is also a repudiation.
>
> Unless the breach makes further performance of the contract impossible for the injured party, the injured party cannot be forced to accept the breach as repudiation but can go on performing the contract.[27]

Therefore, as explained above, when an anticipatory breach occurs, the innocent party may immediately sue for the breach. Alternatively, the innocent party may wait and urge the breaching party to perform. Once the injured party confirms the continuation of the contract, the innocent party cannot later decide to rescind the contract. An example is the case of *Long v Lloyd* [1958] 2 All ER 402. In this case, the plaintiff purchased a vehicle from the defendant. The vehicle had defects, allegedly known to the defendant at the time of the sale. Nonetheless, the plaintiff affirmed the contract after both parties agreed to share the costs of repairs to the vehicle. Subsequently, the vehicle broke down and the plaintiff attempted to rescind the contract. The court found that the plaintiff's previous decision to continue with the contract constituted an affirmation. This affirmation of the contract prevented the plaintiff from later rescinding the agreement.[28]

Damages for the breach of contract generally will be determined on the date of the anticipatory breach. This is the date the plaintiff first learned of the anticipatory breach and had the capability to sue in court. If, for example, a plaintiff buyer substantially delays in suing the defendant seller, then the plaintiff risks adverse price increases during the period of delay. However, anticipatory breach is not an available remedy if the innocent party has fully performed under the contract. The performing party must wait for the future payment date specified in the contract. To avoid this problem, some parties insert an 'acceleration clause' into their agreement. This clause accelerates or makes all future payments due immediately, in the event that one payment instalment is breached. Acceleration clauses can be found in most mortgage contracts. The mortgagee bank fully performs by providing the mortgagor with the full amount of the loan. The mortgagor uses the loan to pay the seller for the flat which the mortgagor is buying. The mortgagor then repays this bank's loan in monthly instalments. Should the mortgagor default on one payment, all the payments become due immediately under the mortgage's acceleration clause.

D. Frustration

A contract is considered to be discharged by *frustration* when performance of the contract becomes impossible due to an unexpected or unforeseen change of the circumstances in which performance is required after the contract was made.[29] Thus, one party's non-performance will not be a breach of contract because the impossibility excuses the performance of the contract.

The change of circumstances must be without fault of either party, and the change makes the circumstances fundamentally different from what was reasonably anticipated by the parties at the time they made the contract.[30] The purpose of the doctrine of frustration is fairness: that it would be unfair to bind the parties to the contract under the new circumstances and under an essentially different bargain.[31]

This principle of contract law has been summarised in the case of *National Carriers Ltd v Panalpina (Northern) Ltd* [1981] AC 675 (HL):

> Frustration of a contract takes place when there . . . [occurs] an event (without default of either party and for which the contract makes no sufficient provision) which so significantly changes the nature (not merely the expense or onerousness) of the outstanding contractual rights and/or obligations from what the parties . . . contemplated at the time of its execution that it would be unjust to hold them to the . . . [contract] in the new circumstances; in such case the law declares both parties to be discharged from further performance.[32]

To determine whether a party may successfully claim frustration of contract, a court will:

- interpret the contract terms in light of the contract's nature and the circumstances at the time of making the contract in order to reveal the scope of the parties' obligations;

- examine the situation after the frustrating event in order to determine the parties' obligations now if their contract is to be enforced; and
- compare the original obligations and the new obligations in order to decide whether the new obligations are radically different from the original obligations.[33]

A claim of frustration of contract may arise from several types of frustrating events:

- physical destruction of the subject matter of the contract
- delay making performance impossible or impracticable by becoming unduly burdensome and the obligations changed radically from that contemplated when the contract was executed
- death or incapacity of the performing party, especially where the original contract is for personal services
- cancellation of an expected event, which was the basis for making the contract (e.g., an agreement to view an event that was subsequently cancelled)
- after the contract was made, subsequent changes in the law which make performance impossible[34]

An example of a claim of frustration of contract arose during the Severe Acute Respiratory Syndrome (SARS) epidemic in Hong Kong. In the case of *Li Ching Wing v Xuan Yi Xiong* [2004] 1 HKC 353, the tenant of a flat in Amoy Gardens attempted and failed to avoid the lease on the basis of frustration as the building in which the flat was located was quarantined by the Hong Kong government during the SARS epidemic. As part of this quarantine, the government isolated the occupants of the building by relocating these residents to remote locations.

The reasons for a claim of frustration cannot be self-induced.[35] In other words, a party cannot make it impossible for itself to perform its contractual obligations. Also note the consequences of frustration provided for under the Law Amendment and Reform (Consolidation) Ordinance (Cap 23) at sections 16 to 18. The fact that the contractual obligations are made more expensive by a change in circumstances does not constitute frustration of a contract.[36]

E. Breach

A *breach* of contract occurs when at least one of the parties to a contract fails to perform its obligation in accordance with the contract terms.[37]

In other words, a party fails to do what it promised to do. In this situation, the party who fails to perform is frequently referred to as the defaulting party or the breaching party. The other party in this situation is frequently referred to as the innocent party, injured party, or non-breaching party.

A breach must be evaluated to determine its effect on the rights and duties of the parties. This is done by reviewing the contract as a whole, considering the parties' intentions as stated in the contract, or as the intentions may be inferred from the contract. A breach may arise in three ways: a repudiation of contract before performance is required, partial performance, or incomplete or improper performance.

A party's failure to honour its contractual promise is a breach of contract. A breach may be of an express term or of an implied term. This broken contractual promise may be a breach of warranty or a breach of condition. As previously discussed in Chapter 4, section B, a breach of warranty only allows the innocent party to claim damages. When the breach is trivial or minor, the other party is to continue with its contractual obligations. A defaulting party's breach of warranty does not give the innocent party a right to terminate the contract.

A breach of condition, however, may allow the innocent party to terminate the contract as well as claim damages because the breach is serious and fundamental to the contract. In this case, the innocent party has a right to terminate the contract. If the innocent party exercises this right, the non-breaching party is excused from fulfilling its obligations under the contract. Additionally, the innocent party may keep any benefit already received, providing that the innocent party terminated the contract as soon as possible and gave notification of the termination. Alternatively, the innocent party may decide to continue the contract rather than terminate the legally binding agreement when a breach of condition occurs. In this case, the breach of condition will be treated as a breach of warranty. In other words, if the innocent party chooses to continue with the contract, the innocent party can only sue for damages resulting from the breach.

As mentioned earlier, anticipatory breach occurs where one party repudiates the contract before the due date of performance, or where some of the contractual obligations remain unperformed. Repudiation may be expressed or implied, e.g., the party states its intention not to perform, or by its conduct indicates its intention not to perform its obligations under the contract.

Under this situation, the innocent party is excused from performing its obligations under the contract and may claim damages. The injured party must *mitigate*, i.e., minimise its losses. Alternatively, the non-breaching party may refuse to accept the breach and confirm the contract's continuing existence, giving the other party an opportunity to change its position before the due date for performance.

7

Damages and Remedies

This chapter reviews what one party may do when the other party to the contract has failed to fulfil its obligations or responsibilities.

> Whether or not a breach of contract gives rise to a right to rescind, it gives the injured party a right of action for damages. . . . The contract may provide for a sum payable as liquidated damages in the event of breach.
>
> In certain cases where damages would be an inadequate remedy application may be made for a decree of specific performance; or, where the obligation is a negative one, for an injunction to restrain breach of the contract. Certain types of contracts may give rise to special remedies, for example the rights of lien and resale under a contract for the sale of goods, or the right of repossession under a contract of hire purchase.[1]

A. Damages

Damages are intended to pay the innocent party for the loss caused by the other party's breach of contract.[2] Damages are intended as compensation for the cost incurred by the innocent party and to place this injured party in the same position as if the contract had been fully performed.[3] In other words, an innocent party cannot make a profit from a claim for damages.[4] Damages generally are decided by the courts using the principle of *remoteness of damage*[5] and the principle of *mitigation of loss*. However, the parties are free to agree in the contract to change or limit the rules for damages. For example, the parties may agree to the use of exemption clauses and liquidated damages, as discussed in Chapter 4, section C, and Chapter 7, section B, respectively.

i. Principles of Damages

The principle of remoteness of damage provides that the innocent party can recover those losses which are naturally related to the breach, or losses which could arise and which were in the parties' reasonable contemplation at the time they made the contract.[6] The defaulting party will be liable for losses outside the natural course of events where the circumstances which caused the loss were known to the defaulting party at the time of making the contract.

The case of *Hadley v Baxendale* (1854) 9 Ex 341 first stated the remoteness of damage principle. This case involved a mill. Due to a broken crankshaft, the mill's operation came to a stop. The defendant carriers failed to deliver the broken crankshaft to the manufacturer for repairs within the time promised. As a result, the plaintiff sued for loss of profits due to the delay. The plaintiff lost the case as the defendant's knowledge was insufficient to 'show reasonably that the profits of the mill must be stopped by an unreasonable delay in the delivery of the broken shaft by the carriers to the third person'.[7] In other words, the defendant did not know of the plaintiff's particular situation: that the plaintiff only had one crankshaft when it was usual for mills to have spare crankshafts available for use while a broken crankshaft is being repaired.

The principle of mitigation requires the injured party to take all reasonable steps to minimise the loss resulting from the other party's breach, before making a claim for damages.

> There are three rules often referred to under the comprehensive heading of "mitigation" . . . First, the claimant cannot recover damages for any part of his loss consequent upon the defendant's breach of contract that the claimant could have avoided by taking reasonable steps. Secondly, if the claimant in fact avoids or mitigates his loss consequent upon the defendant's breach, he cannot recover for such avoided loss, even though the steps he took were more than could be reasonably required of him under the first rule. Thirdly, where the claimant incurs loss or expense in the course of taking reasonable steps to mitigate the loss resulting from the defendant's breach, the claimant may recover this further loss or expense from the defendant.[8]

Another aspect concerning mitigation is that the determination whether a loss was avoidable is a question of fact rather than a question of law. As the Court of Appeal stated in the case of *Mega Yield International Holdings v Fonfair Co Ltd* [2014] HKEC 1546:

> the question what is reasonable for a person to do in mitigation of his damages cannot be a question of law but must be one of fact in the circumstances of each particular case and is a conclusion arrived at on a consideration of all the circumstances of the case.[9]

ii. Types of Damages

There are different types of damages that a court may award the innocent party in a successful claim in contract law.[10] The most common type of damages made for breaches of contract is *expectation damages*. The courts determine the profits that would have been made if the contract had been fully completed. This method places the injured party in the same financial position as if the contract had been fully performed. Damages are normally determined at the time of the breach for the loss of value to the innocent party. The courts would consider the value that the injured party should have received under the terms of the contract, the actual value received by that party, and any incidental and foreseeable consequential damages. The courts would also reduce the damages by any expenses that the innocent party would have had to incur to fully perform that contract.[11]

In some circumstances where determining the amount of expectation damages is difficult, the courts may instead award *reliance damages* for breaches of contract.[12] Reliance damages seek to compensate the innocent party for expenses incurred in performing the breached contract and do not include lost profits. Thus, reliance damages place the injured party back to its original position, as if the contract had never been made. The courts may also award reliance damages where a party has incurred detrimental reliance from an unenforceable agreement.

The courts may also award *restitution damages* for partially performed contracts.[13] Restitution damages are claimable when the defaulting party obtained a benefit from the innocent party's partial performance of the contract. The determination of restitution damages is normally based on the market value of the services performed, e.g., the price to obtain similar performance in the market. Alternatively, the damages may be determined by the amount to which the services performed increased the value of the defaulting party's property. Where there is a choice, a court would award the higher amount. A court award of restitution damages is to prevent an unfair benefit to the defaulting party by forcing that party to pay the injured party for the value of any performance that the defaulting party received. Restitution damages do not seek to enforce the contract.

In rare circumstances, courts may exercise discretion in awarding *nominal damages* or *punitive damages*. Nominal damages are awarded when the innocent party proves a breach of contract claim against the defaulting party but fails to prove any damages.[14] Punitive damages are awarded to punish the defaulting party and to deter others from similar reprehensible conduct, rather than to compensate the injured party.[15] Punitive damages are generally not available for a breach of contract unless the conduct of the defaulting party is considered so morally unacceptable by the courts as to justify punitive damages.[16]

B. Liquidated Damages

Liquidated damages are the agreed sums which the parties specified in the contract as the damages to be paid to the innocent party if a breach occurs.[17] Liquidated damages clauses are included in contracts to avoid the difficulty and expense of proving damages. To be enforceable, the liquidated damages must be a genuine pre-estimate of loss; the amount stated in the clause must have a reasonable relationship to any probable loss. A genuine pre-estimate of loss will be enforced even if it turns out to be higher or lower than the actual loss.[18]

This is to be contrasted with penalty clauses, which are not enforceable. Penalty clauses provide for compensation amounts *in terrorem*, i.e., threatening, to the party in breach. Nevertheless, should a court void a liquidated damages clause because it is in fact a penalty, the breaching party can still be sued for damages if the innocent party proves those damages. The existence of a liquidated damages clause in the contract does not necessarily exclude injunctive relief or specific performance unless the contract explicitly states that the exclusive remedy is damages.[19]

The distinctions between liquidated damages and penalties were considered in *Dunlop Pneumatic Tyre Co v New Garage Co* [1915] AC 79, from which the following principles may be deduced:

- The labels which the parties attach to the clauses are not conclusive.
- Whether a pre-agreed sum is a penalty or liquidated damages is to be determined by the circumstances at the time of the making of the contract.
- A pre-agreed sum is a penalty if the amount is extravagant and unconscionable in comparison with the greatest loss conceivable.
- A pre-agreed sum is a penalty if the breach is a default of payment and the stipulated sum is higher than the defaulted payment.
- If a single sum is to be applied to various breaches with different degrees of seriousness, it is likely to be a penalty.[20]

The Supreme Court of Canada observed in *Elsley v J G Collins Insurance Agencies Ltd* (1978) 83 DLR (3d) 1:

> It is now evident that the power to strike down a penalty clause is a blatant interference with freedom of contract and it is designed for the sole purpose of providing relief against oppression for the party having to pay the stipulated sum. It has no place where there is no oppression.[21]

The court in *Philips Hong Kong Ltd v Attorney General of Hong Kong* (1993) 61 BLR 49 (PC) approved of this decision. Thus, where there is equal bargaining power between the parties, the court will not readily invalidate a stipulated sum as a penalty. In the case of *Polyset Ltd v Panhandat Ltd* [2000] 4 HKC 203 (CA), the Hong Kong Court of Appeal held that a forfeiture of deposit up to 35 per cent of the purchase price in a land sale was not a penalty. This is because the parties had equal bargaining power and the amount was not out of proportion to the possible loss if the property market suddenly dropped, which was likely in the circumstances of the case.

C. Specific Performance

What if monetary damages (liquidated or unliquidated) is for some reason inadequate or inappropriate? Equity provides an additional remedy known as *specific performance*.[22] An order of specific performance by a court would require a defaulting party to perform specifically according to the terms of the contract. This equitable remedy is for cases where the contract's subject matter is considered to be unique, such as the situation with land or irreplaceable items. In these circumstances, the damages paid as compensation would be inadequate.[23] In showing the inadequacy of damages, the injured party may show that an accurate determination of damages would be too uncertain or too difficult to be assessed.

Specific performance is discretionary upon the courts. In deciding whether to grant specific performance, the courts will weigh the relative hardship on each party if specific performance is or is not granted. The injured party seeking specific performance must have *clean hands*, i.e., must have acted in good faith, without any wrongdoing, or moral fault or blame.[24] The innocent party must claim specific performance without delay, as delay would prevent the claim for equitable remedies.[25] Specific performance also requires consideration for the contract. Consideration must be present.[26] Specific performance will not be granted in the following situations:

- A contract lacks mutuality even though the contract is made under seal. In other words, the remedy of specific performance must be available to both parties at the time the contract was made and there must be consideration rather than a seal.[27]
- A court would find it impossible to supervise the performance of the contract, e.g., where one party is bound by continuous duties, the performance of which might require constant court supervision.[28]
- The contract is too vague.[29]
- It is a contract of personal service, e.g., an employment contract.[30]
- The result would impose severe hardship upon the defendant.[31]

D. Restrictions on Remedies

There can be limitations on the remedies that can be claimed by an injured party. For example, an innocent party may be limited in the type or the amount of damages which can be claimed for a breach of contract. These limitations might be imposed by the parties themselves or these limitations can be imposed by law. We start first with a review of party-imposed limitations before proceeding to legal limitations.

As mentioned, limitations on remedies may be agreed between the parties under their contract. The following are some examples of these restrictions which may be imposed by the parties to the contract. The first example is liquidated damages. As noted earlier, liquidated damages arise where the parties, at the time of entering into a contract, have included in the agreement the price of a breach of the contract. The courts will only examine whether the parties, at the time of making the contract, made a genuine pre-estimate of the loss. The courts will not determine the accuracy of the estimate. Again, note that a liquidated damages clause cannot be used as a penalty clause. Penalty clauses are void as the parties to a contract are not permitted to impose punitive or unconscionable sanctions on each other.[32]

Another illustration of party-imposed restrictions is the use of a deposit. The function of a deposit is similar to liquidated damages, except that a deposit is usually required at the commencement of the contract. With a deposit, some consideration, generally money, is paid in advance and can be forfeited if the party making the deposit fails to proceed with the contract. Deposits may be considered as a type of a guarantee of performance.[33]

A final example of party-imposed restriction on recovery of damages is the limitation clause or exemption clause. Using this type of clause, one party to the contract attempts to exclude, exempt, or limit liability for which that party may be responsible. Exemption clauses were discussed earlier.[34]

An example of the legal restrictions upon an innocent party to recover for a breach concerns the common law doctrine of privity. The rules and the law governing the transaction are made by the parties to a contract; therefore, only those parties are bound by the responsibilities and receive the benefits of the contract. Thus, only parties to a contract may sue on that contract. However, this doctrine of privity might be avoided by finding the existence of a collateral contract. A party not involved in the main contract may sue one of the parties to the main contract under the collateral contract, thereby indirectly enforcing the main contract.

This is demonstrated in the following case. In *Shanklin Pier v Detel Products* [1951] 2 KB 854, the plaintiff owned a pier. The defendant manufactured paint and made a statement to the plaintiff that its paint would last for approximately ten years. The plaintiff instructed its contractor to purchase the paint from the defendant. The contractor bought the paint and used it to paint the plaintiff's pier. The paint lasted three months. As the main contract for the paint's purchase was between the contractor and the defendant, the plaintiff had no privity of contract with the defendant. The court determined that a collateral contract existed between the plaintiff and the defendant. The consideration for this collateral contract was the plaintiff's instruction to its contractor to purchase the paint based upon the defendant's promise of the paint's durability.

As discussed earlier, Hong Kong has implemented the Contracts (Rights of Third Parties) Ordinance (Cap 623) which gives some legal rights in certain situations to third parties, thus restricting the application of the common law doctrine of privity. Some other examples of the statutorily imposed restrictions on liability include the Control of Exemption Clauses Ordinance (Cap 71), Misrepresentation Ordinance (Cap 284) and the Sale of Goods Ordinance (Cap 26), all of which have been mentioned earlier.

Another example of a statutorily imposed restriction on an injured party's recovery is the Limitation Ordinance (Cap 347). This ordinance is a statute of limitations which does not allow a particular remedy after a specified time. For lawsuits concerning simple contracts, the limitation period is six years from the date on which the reason to sue arises. If the contract is under seal, i.e., a deed, the limitation period is twelve years.

The cause of action, i.e., the right to sue, generally arises or begins at the time of a breach or when the cause of action was discovered or should have been discovered. No lawsuit may be brought after the limitation period expires.[35]

At the end of the time limit, the remedy becomes time-barred but the injured party's rights under the contract remain. For example, a time-barred debt remains payable. A creditor cannot sue on the debt to recover payment. However, should the debtor make a payment to the creditor to whom both time-barred and current debts are owed, without designating to which debt the payment should be allocated, the creditor may allocate the payment to the time-barred debt.[36]

Notes

Chapter 1

1. See Michael J. Fisher and Desmond G. Greenwood, *Contract Law in Hong Kong* (2nd edition, 2011) 7 [hereinafter *Fisher and Greenwood*]. For a discussion of the topic of employment, see 24 *Halsbury's Laws of Hong Kong* (2nd edition, 2012).
2. The Hong Kong Government's Bilingual Laws Information System's *The English-Chinese Glossary of Legal Terms* [hereinafter *BLIS Glossary*] translates *common law* as 普通法 and *common law jurisdiction* as 普通法司法管轄區. See the *BLIS Glossary* website at: http://www.legislation.gov.hk/eng/glossary/homeglos.htm.
3. H. G. Beale et al., eds., *1 Chitty on Contracts* para. 1-016 (31st edition, 2012) [hereinafter *Chitty*]; Betty M. Ho and Stephen Hall, *Ho and Hall's Hong Kong Contract Law* 2 (3rd edition, 2013) [hereinafter *Ho*].
4. *Chitty* at para. 1-016; *Butterworths Hong Kong Contract Law Handbook* (3rd edition, 2013) 8 [hereinafter *Butterworths*].
5. *Chitty* at para. 1-018.
6. See id.
7. See id. at para. 1-020.
8. See, e.g., *Fisher and Greenwood* at 1 which defines a contract as a legally enforceable agreement.
9. 18 *Halsbury's Laws of Hong Kong* (2nd edition, 2015 reissue) para. 115.002 [hereinafter 18 *Halsbury's*].
10. The *BLIS Glossary* translates *legal contracts* as 合法合同 and *legally binding* as 具法律約束力.
11. Richard Stone and James Devenney, *The Modern Law of Contract* (11th edition, 2015) 312–13 [hereinafter *Stone*].
12. Carole Chui and Derek Roebuck, *Hong Kong Contracts* (2nd edition, 1991) paras. 1.3, 2.1 [hereinafter *Chui and Roebuck*].

Chapter 2

1. See 18 *Halsbury's* at paras. 115.011–115.012.
2. *Chitty* at para. 1-087 notes that contracts: 'may be classified in a variety of ways: according to their subject-matter; according to their parties; according to their form (whether contained in deeds or in writing, whether express or implied) or according to their effect (whether bilateral or unilateral, whether valid, void, voidable or unenforceable)'.

   This work is not intended to examine these categories in such depth; only the more common types or categories of contract will be introduced. For a detailed discussion of the myriad of contract types, see, e.g., id. at paras. 1-088–1-104.
3. 18 *Halsbury's* at para. 115.010.
4. The *BLIS Glossary* translates *recognisance* as 擔保.
5. 18 *Halsbury's* at para. 115.010.
6. Id. at para. 115.013.
7. *Chitty* at para. 1-099.
8. 18 *Halsbury's* at para. 115.054 explains that the mode of acceptance in a unilateral contract: 'is performance of his side of the contract by the offeree. . . . the real distinction between bilateral and unilateral contracts lies not in the nature of the act of acceptance, but in whether there is a contract before performance of that act; in a bilateral contract there will be an executory promise by the offeree, but in a unilateral contract the promise will be executed the moment it is made. . . . In the case of a unilateral contract, performance of his side of the contract constitutes acceptance by the offeree.'
9. *Chui and Roebuck* at para. 4.8: 'The word collateral in this context simply indicates a contract which exists alongside a main contract. For instance, a contract of guarantee cannot exist without something to guarantee.' *Collateral* means *running side by side*. The consideration for a collateral contract is entering into the main contract in return for a collateral assurance. *Fisher and Greenwood* at 166.
10. *Chui and Roebuck* at para. 9.2.6; *Fisher and Greenwood* at 166.
11. 18 *Halsbury's* at para. 115.140 explains a collateral contract as a: 'contract between A and B may be accompanied by a collateral contract between B and C, whereby C makes a promise to B in return for B entering into the contract with A or doing some other act for the benefit of C'.
12. *Stone* at 176–77.
13. Id. at 197.
14. *Chitty* at para. 18-003. Id. at para. 18-021 states further: 'The common law doctrine of privity means . . . that a person cannot acquire rights, or be subjected to liabilities, *arising under* a contract to which he is not a party. For example, it means that, if A promises B to pay a sum of money to C, then C cannot sue A for that sum.' See also *Butterworths* at 75–77.

15. *Fisher and Greenwood* at 435. For a full discussion of this topic, see, e.g., id. at Chapter 16 ('Privity of Contract'); *Chitty* at Chapter 18 ('Third Parties'); *Ho* at Chapter 13 ('Privity').
16. *Fisher and Greenwood* at 443–45.
17. The consultation paper may be found at the following two websites: http://www.hkreform.gov.hk or http://www.hklii.org/hk/hklrc/reports/2005/3.doc. See *Fisher and Greenwood* at 444–49 for a review of the consultation paper.
18. The commission's report may be found at the following two web sites: http://www.hkreform.gov.hk or http://www.hklii.org/hk/hklrc/reports/2005/10/privity_of_contract.3.doc.
19. There are several items of note about this ordinance:
    - This law does not apply to certain agreements such as promissory notes, deeds of mutual covenant, or contracts of carriage.
    - The parties can specifically provide in their contract that this law does not apply to their agreement (section 4(3)).
    - Under certain situations, however, the parties might not be able to include in their contract a provision to remove the third party's rights (section 6).
    - In defending a claim for breach of contract, the offending party has against the third party the same defences as it does against the innocent party (section 8).
    - In defending a claim for breach of contract, the offending party is not liable both to the innocent party and to the third party (section 11).
20. The *BLIS Glossary* translates *deed* as 契據. See also *Ho* at 153–57.
21. See Chapter 3, section C and the accompanying footnotes. See also 18 *Halsbury's* at para. 115.011. The *BLIS Glossary* translates *specialty* as 蓋印文據.
22. *Black's Law Dictionary* (7th edition, 1999) 1350 [hereinafter *Black's Law Dictionary*] defines *seal* to be an 'impression or sign that has legal consequence when applied to an instrument'.
23. *Chitty* at para. 1-093.
24. Another reason for using a deed is that the party suffering a loss caused by a breach, i.e., the failure to follow the terms of the agreement, has a longer period in which to sue the breaching party.
25. *Chui and Roebuck* at para. 2.2.
26. Conveyancing and Property Ordinance (Cap 219) section 4(2).
27. Powers of Attorney Ordinance (Cap 31) section 2(2).

Chapter 3

1. See, e.g., *Charles Wild and Stuart Weinstein, Smith and Keenan's English Law: Text and Cases* (16th edition, 2010) 288.

2. 18 *Halsbury's* at para. 115.031.
3. *Black's Law Dictionary* at 1111. See also *Butterworths* at 13.
4. See *Ho* at 6.
5. Marnah Suff, *Essential Contract Law* (2nd edition, 1997) 2 [hereinafter *Suff*].
6. See *Ho* at 21–22, 27–28.
7. *Suff* at 2. See also *Ho* at 21–22, 27–28.
8. *Fisher and Greenwood* at 71–73. See M. P. Furmston, ed., *Cheshire, Fifoot and Furmston's Law of Contract* (16th edition, 2012) 77–80 [hereinafter *Furmston*].
9. *Lee Siu Fong Mary v Ngai Yee Chai* [2006] 1 HKC 157, 161 (citations omitted).
10. The topic of *collateral contract* is discussed in Chapter 2, section D. *Black's Law Dictionary* at 319 defines this term as: 'A side agreement that relates to a contract . . . an agreement made before or at the same time as, but separately from, another contract.'
11. *Chitty* at para. 2-027. See also *Butterworths* at 26–34.
12. See 18 *Halsbury's* at paras. 115.078–115.088; *Butterworths* at 26–34; *Chitty* at paras. 2-048–2-050.
13. 18 *Halsbury's* at para. 115.082 notes: 'Ordinarily, a letter is not "posted" until it is put in a Post Office letter box. Thus, the delivery of a letter to a postman outside the course of his ordinary duties is not a posting of the letter, nor will such a letter be assumed to be in the lawful custody of the Post Office as soon as the postman enters the post office.' Thus, the acceptance of an offer must be placed in the: 'control of the Post Office or of one of its employees authorised to *receive* letters. Handing letters to a postman authorised to *deliver* letters is not posting.' *Chitty* at para. 2-048 (emphasis in original).
14. For discussion on the application of the postal rule to telegrams, see 18 *Halsbury's* at para. 115.087.
15. Id. at para. 115-079. *Fisher and Greenwood* at 65 states: 'Email may be thought of as being an instantaneous communication. However, this is not strictly the case, as a message will have to pass through at least one server to reach its target destination. The sender knows that the recipient will only check his mail inbox from time to time. This means there will usually be a delay before it is read. Similarly, with telephone answering machines, the sender knows that the message has not been instantaneously received by the offeror. . . . given that the courts have shown a reluctance to extend the postal rule to other areas, it is far more likely that emails and similar will be viewed as subject to the normal rules; acceptance taking effect when and where notice of acceptance is received.'
16. In relation to acceptance by e-mails, see the Electronic Transactions Ordinance (Cap 553) which makes it clear that acceptance by e-mail will be effective only when received, unless the parties have agreed otherwise.
17. *Chitty* at para. 2-051.

18. *Susanto-Wing Sun Co Ltd v Yung Chi Hardware Machinery Co Ltd* [1989] 2 HKC 504, 506.

19. *Stevenson, Jaques & Co v McLean* (1880) 5 QBD 346, 350.

20. Id.

21. *Chitty* at paras. 2-008 and 2-010. See also *Ho* at 18–20.

22. 18 *Halsbury's* at para. 115.033. This authority continues by saying: 'a distinction must be drawn between those declarations which amount to offers, and those which only amount to invitations to treat. Sometimes, a particular type of declaration is, at least *prima facie*, put into one or the other category by statute or by common law; but in all other cases it is a question of intention. An express statement that a declaration is not an offer is effective to prevent it being an offer.' Id.

23. Display of goods in a shop window has been held to be an invitation to treat. See, e.g., *Fisher v Bell* [1961] 1 QB 394 where the court decided that the display of a knife in the shop's window was an invitation to treat. If the display were an offer, the shopkeeper would have been in violation of the Restriction of Offensive Weapons Act 1959. A similar situation arose in the earlier case of *Pharmaceutical Society of Great Britain v Boots Cash Chemists (Southern) Ltd* [1953] 1 QB 401:

> the customer was allowed to select goods from the shelves and take them to the cash desk. By the desk was a registered pharmacist who could prevent the removal of certain drugs from the store. The defendants were alleged to be in breach of an English statute which said there must be a registered pharmacist to 'supervise sale'. The main issue in the case was whether or not the display of goods on the shelves of the self-service store was an offer or an invitation to treat. If the display was an offer, then the taking of the goods from the shelf by the customer and putting them in his basket would, it was alleged, constitute an acceptance. The sale would, therefore, take place without the requisite supervision and so an offence would be committed under the statute. The court held that the display amounted only to an invitation to treat.
>
> The court reasoned that if the plaintiff was correct the customer, once he had placed the goods in his basket, could not then change his mind and substitute the goods for other goods without being liable to pay for the goods originally chosen. This would be commercially disastrous for self-service stores as customers would be too afraid to patronise them.
>
> A further explanation of the 'invitation only' finding was that the shopkeeper should have right to refuse to sell the goods to a customer since shops are, theoretically, places to bargain.

See *Fisher and Greenwood* at 46–47.

24. *Ho* at 15.

25. *Chitty* at para. 2-008.
26. Id. at para. 2-010.
27. 35 *Halsbury's Laws of Hong Kong* para. 230.148 (2nd edition, 2013) (citing *Lobley Co Ltd v Tsang Yuk Kiu* [1997] 2 HKC 442; *Blackpool and Fylde Aero Club v Blackpool Borough Council* [1990] 1 WLR 1195; *City Polytechnic of Hong Kong v Blue Cross (Asia-Pacific) Insurance Ltd* [1994] 3 HKC 423; *City University of Hong Kong v Blue Cross (Asia-Pacific) Insurance Ltd* [2001] 1 HKC 463).
28. *Currie v Misa* (1875) LR 10 Ex 153, 162.
29. *Dunlop Pneumatic Tyre Co v Selfridge & Co* [1915] AC 847, 855.
30. Consideration can be categorised as *executed* and *executory*. As explained in *Ho* at 93: 'Executed consideration consists of performance (or forbearance) of the required act constituting the price for the promise, e.g., the return of a lost item (for a reward or promise thereof). Executory consideration consists of a promise, express or implied, to perform (or forbear from performing) the required act, e.g., promise of a reward (for the return of a lost item).'

    Fisher and Greenwood at 89 states: 'It is generally the case that "executory" consideration is just as valuable as "executed" consideration: i.e. the promise of an act is as effective as the act itself. For example, if a seller of goods fails to deliver them on time, the buyer has a right to sue even though the goods have not yet been paid for. Executory consideration exists in the buyer's promise to pay for the goods when required to do so. Provided that the buyer has not indicated that he is no longer willing or able to proceed he is entitled to sue the seller for the latter's non-delivery. In cases of "unilateral" contracts, where only one party has undertaken obligations, the promisee's consideration can only exist in an act rather than a promise, since he gives no promise. Mrs. Carlill, for example, did not make any promises to the Carbolic Smoke Ball Co. Her consideration existed in the *act* of using the ball as directed; it was, in other words, executed rather than executory.'

    For further discussion, see, e.g., 18 *Halsbury's* at paras. 115.117 and 115.121. The *BLIS Glossary* translates *consideration* as 代價.
31. *Thomas v Thomas* (1842) 2 QB 851, 859.
32. 18 *Halsbury's* at para. 115.117. Consideration for a promise may consist in either some benefit for the promisor, or some disadvantage incurred by the promisee, or both. Id.
33. Id. at para. 115.126 states: 'Whilst consideration need not be adequate it must be of some value. It has been settled that the following are no consideration: past consideration; a promise to do an act which is obviously impossible, or which has no legal effect; a promise which does not involve any legal obligation; or, possibly, a promise which is illegal or void.'

    Fisher and Greenwood at 83 notes:

    > The rule is that "Consideration must be 'sufficient' (of some value) but need not be 'adequate' (of equal value to the other party's

> consideration).” There is nothing wrong, in consideration terms, with an agreement to buy a valuable painting for $10 . . .
>
> Consideration is, essentially, a token of a party's intention to make a legally binding contract as opposed, for example, to a non-binding social arrangement. That token takes the form of the giving of something valuable in the eyes of the law. Consideration may not prove that a bargain is fair or equal but it *is* evidence of a legally enforceable contract, as opposed to a mere friendly arrangement never intended to be contractual. (emphasis in original)

For a further discussion on this topic of sufficiency of consideration, see, e.g., *Furmston* at 108–44.

34. See, e.g., *Thomas v Thomas* (1842) 2 QB 851. See also *Butterworths* at 39–43.
35. *Chitty* at para. 3-014 (emphasis in original). See also 18 *Halsbury's* at para. 115.124. The *BLIS Glossary* translates *valuable consideration* as 有值代價.
36. *Chitty* at para. 3-022.
37. Id. at paras. 3-039–3-040. See also *Ho* at 122–25, 127–29.
38. *Fisher and Greenwood* at 89 (emphasis in original).
39. *Pao On v Lau Yiu Long* [1980] AC 614, 629 (PC).
40. For present purposes, consider *economic duress* to refer to unfair business pressure. Economic duress is discussed in Chapter 5, section B.iii.
41. *Williams v Roffey Bros* [1991] 1 QB 1, 15–16.
42. See, e.g., the discussion in *Fisher and Greenwood* at 99–105.
43. *UBC (Construction) Ltd v Sung Foo Kee Ltd* [1993] 2 HKLR 207.
44. The *BLIS Glossary* translates *equity* as 衡平法 and *equitable remedy* as 衡平法補救. *Equitable relief* may be translated as 衡平法濟助.
45. The *BLIS Glossary* translates *estoppel* as 不容反悔法. Some sources refer to this doctrine as *promissory estoppel*. 18 *Halsbury's* at para. 115.394 describes this doctrine:

> Similar to waiver is the doctrine of promissory or equitable estoppel, whereby a party who has represented that he will not insist upon his strict rights under the contract will not be allowed to resile from that position, or will be allowed to do so only upon giving reasonable notice. This principle differs from estoppel properly so called in that (1) it applies to promises, not representations of fact; (2) it is generally only suspensory in operation; and (3) it is not clear to what extent the representee need have changed his position to his detriment in reliance on the representation.

A party's waiver of the right to fully enforce all the terms of a contract is an intentional abandonment of a contractual right. The waiver of a promise or condition may be expressed or may be implied from a party's conduct.

46. As stated in 44 *Halsbury's Laws of Hong Kong* para. 340.110 (2nd edition, 2011) [hereinafter 44 *Halsbury's*]:

> Estoppel at law arises where one person makes to another a clear and unequivocal representation of existing fact with knowledge of its falsehood and with the intention that it should be acted upon. In some circumstances, failure to speak or act may amount to a representation, if there is a duty to speak or act owed to the other person. If, in these circumstances, the person to whom the representation is made acts upon it to his detriment, the person making it may not thereafter assert in any proceedings which may arise that the facts were otherwise than as he represented them to be.
>
> Equitable estoppel is more flexible, both in its initial requirements and also in its consequences, than estoppel at law. Equitable estoppel takes two forms: proprietary estoppel . . . and promissory estoppel. . . . it has been suggested that there is one simple synthesis of both forms to the effect that it would be unconscionable for a party to be permitted to deny that which, knowingly or unknowingly, he has allowed another to assume to his detriment.

47. This involves a representation of some type or kind. 18 *Halsbury's* at para. 115.396: 'The basis of promissory estoppel is that one party has been led by the conduct of the other to believe that that other's strict rights under the contract will not be enforced. . . . a promissory estoppel can only be founded upon a clear and unambiguous promise of future action.' Again, for equitable estoppel to apply, there must be a representation by one party to the contract which is relied upon by the other party to the contract to its detriment. Id. at para. 115.397.

48. *Fisher and Greenwood* at 114. In the case of *Dixie Engineering Company Ltd v Vernaltex Company Ltd (t/a Wing Wo Engineering Company)* [2003] HKCU 136, para. 81, the Court of Appeal stated:

> Broken down into its component parts, the doctrine of equitable or promissory estoppel, insofar as it applies in contractual situations, consists of:
>
> (1) A clear and unequivocal representation by A to B that he will not rely on his strict contractual rights. The representation may be by words or by conduct.
> (2) The representation by A must be made with the intention by him "or at least the knowledge" that B will act on it.
> (3) B must in fact have acted in reliance on the representation.

49. The operation of equitable estoppel:

> Like waiver, a concession amounting to a promissory estoppel will generally only suspend the strict legal rights of the party granting it; and he may revert to these rights upon giving reasonable notice of his intention to the other party. . . .
>
> A concession taking effect as a promissory estoppel may, however, become permanently binding and extinguish an obligation

> if it ceases to be possible for the representee to revert to his original position.

18 *Halsbury's* at para. 115.398.

50. *Fisher and Greenwood* at 115.
51. *British Russian Gazette and Trade Outlook Ltd v Associated Newspapers Ltd* [1933] 2 KB 616, 643–44. Both 18 *Halsbury's* at para. 115.404 and *Chitty* at para. 22-012 use this definition for the term *accord and satisfaction*.
52. 18 *Halsbury's* at para. 115.405. Exceptions to this general rule are set out in id.
53. *Chitty* at paras. 22-016–22-017. Id. at para. 22-016 explains in relation to the partial payment of a debt: 'Where there is a claim for a liquidated sum, the liability for which is not in dispute, the acceptance of a smaller sum in satisfaction does not relieve the debtor for there is no consideration for the creditor's abandonment of the balance. This rule, which is generally known as the rule in *Pinnel's Case*, is nevertheless subject to a number of qualifications.'
54. The *BLIS Glossary* translates *compromise* as 妥協.
55. See generally Bankruptcy Ordinance (Cap 6) on voluntary arrangement. Section 2 of this ordinance states in part: '"voluntary arrangement" (自願安排) means a composition in satisfaction of a debtor's debts or a scheme of arrangement of a debtor's affairs.'
56. 18 *Halsbury's* at para. 115.409.
57. There is a particular type of contract known as a *specialty contract*, *contract under seal* or *deed* where consideration is not required. 'A deed is a document which takes its effect from its formal nature.' *Chui and Roebuck* at para. 11.1. *Chitty* at para. 1-105 states:

    > At common law, contracts under seal, or specialties, were an important example of deeds and at common law a deed was an instrument which was not merely in writing, but which was sealed by the party bound thereby, and delivered by him to or for the benefit of the person to whom the liability was incurred. In no other way than by the use of this form could validity be given . . . At common law, all deeds were documents under seal, but not all documents under seal were and are deeds. A deed must either:
    > (a) effect the transference of an interest, right or property;
    > (b) create an obligation binding on some person or persons;
    > (c) confirm some act whereby an interest, right or property has already passed.

58. 18 *Halsbury's* at para. 115.016: 'The only contracts which are required by the rules of common law to be made by deed are contracts made without valuable consideration.' Id. at para. 115.011: 'A promise made by deed . . . derives its validity from its form alone; it is regarded as binding at common law even without consideration, except where void, for example as being in restraint of trade, or illegal. Conveyances of land or of any interest in land must be made by deed.'

59. *Chitty* at para. 1-113 expounds upon this requirement of delivery: 'It remains the case . . . that "[w]here a contract is to be by deed, there must be a delivery to perfect it". "Delivered", however, in this connection does not mean "handed over" to the other party. It means delivered in the old legal sense, namely, an act done so as to evince an intention to be bound. Any act of the party which shows that he intended to deliver the deed as an instrument binding on him is enough. He must make it his deed and recognise it as presently binding on him. Delivery is effective even though the grantor retains the deed in his own possession. There need be no actual transfer of possession to the other party.' See also *Ho* at 154–57.

60. Concerning agreements contained in a deed, the rule is that: 'equity never favoured voluntary transactions even if they were contained in a deed, and refused to grant its special remedies in cases where these were without consideration. So it has been laid down that specific performance will not be decreed of a contract contained in a deed which is entirely without consideration.' *Chitty* at para. 1-128.

61. See id. at paras. 3-021 and 27-030. See Chapter 7, section C, on the subject of *specific performance*. The *BLIS Glossary* translates *injunction* as 禁制令 or 強制令.

62. *Collier v P & M J Wright (Holdings) Ltd* [2008] 1 WLR 643, 659.

Chapter 4

1. 18 *Halsbury's* at para. 115.073. See, e.g., the following cases which analysed whether a contract existed and, if so, its interpretation: *Kabushiki Kaisha Proje Holdings v King Power Group (Hong Kong) Ltd* [2013] HKEC 1574; *Links Internatioinal* [sic] *Relocations Ltd v Swift Christopher Lee* [2013] HKEC 1678.

2. *Professional Associates v Polytek Engineering Co Ltd* [1986] HKLR 20, 34.

3. *Chitty* at para. 12-001.

4. *Pacific Dunlop Garments Ltd v Fundamental Global Ltd* [2014] HKEC 609 (CA), para. 25.

5. Id. at para. 36.

6. *Fully Profit (Asia) Ltd v Secretary for Justice* (2013) 16 HKCFAR 351 (CFA), 361–62.

7. 18 *Halsbury's* at para. 115.154.

8. See id. at para. 115.156; *Chitty* at Chapter 13 ('Implied Term'); Kim Lewison, *The Interpretation of Contracts* (5th edition, 2011) 269–70 [hereinafter *Lewison*].

9. *Fisher and Greenwood* at 168.

10. Id. at 171 citing to *Attorney General v Melhado Investments Ltd* [1983] HKLR 327, 329; *Shun Shing Hing Investment Co Ltd v Attorney General* [1983] HKLR 432, 440; *On Park Parking Ltd v Secretary of Justice* [2004] 3 HKC 476. See also the comments of the Court of Final Appeal in *Sinoearn International*

Ltd v Hyundai-CCECC Joint Venture (2013) 16 HKCFAR 632 that courts generally should adopt a 'business common sense' approach to contract interpretation. Having said that, the court stated that: 'in determining the meaning of the language of a commercial contract, the law generally favours a commercially sensible construction . . . In this case, I do not think commercial common sense provided an answer. . . . there is no support in the language of the contractual documents for the Court of Appeal's conclusion, language over which . . . [the parties] had control. There is no relevant commercial common sense which would enable the court to override the language used [in the contract].' Id. at 660–61.

11. For the avoidance of confusion, the definition provided by *Chitty* at para. 12-025 is adopted:

> The word "condition" is sometimes used . . . to mean simply "a stipulation, a provision" and not to connote a condition in the technical sense of that word. . . . The most commonly used sense of the word "condition" is that of an essential stipulation of the contract which one party guarantees is true or promises will be fulfilled. Any breach of such a stipulation entitles the innocent party, if he so chooses, to treat himself as discharged from further performance of the contract, and notwithstanding that he has suffered no prejudice by the breach. He can also claim damages for any loss suffered.

There are two uses of the word *condition* in contract law. A condition of the type discussed above can be regarded as a promise, the breach of which allows the innocent party to sue. This meaning is different from that of a *contingent condition* [或有的]. If a contract requires an event to occur, but no party promises that the event will occur, then it is a contingent condition to the party's performance under the contract. The contingent condition is a provision that on the happening of some event an obligation or the contract shall come into force. This contingent condition is termed a *condition precedent* [先決條件]. For example, a building contract can be agreed by the parties but is made contingent upon the government's issuance of permits. The issuance of the government permits is the condition precedent. Once the permits are issued, the condition is met and a legally binding agreement comes into effect.

See, e.g., id. at paras. 12-026–12-029. A related concept is a *condition subsequent* [後決條件]. A provision may provide that an obligation or the contract is ended, without any fault of either party, if a condition does not continue to be satisfied. Thus, if the specified condition subsequent occurs, the contract is ended. A party may waive this condition if it is inserted solely for the party's own benefit. This is demonstrated in the case of:

> *Head v Tattersall* where A bought a horse from B which B warranted to have been hunted with the Bicester hounds. If it did not answer its description, A was to have the right to return it by a certain day. The horse did not answer its description and A accordingly returned it before the day. In the meantime, however, the horse had been

> injured without A's fault. It was held that the injury did not cause A to lose his right to return the horse and he could recover the purchase price paid.

Chitty at para. 12-030. The *BLIS Glossary* translates *contingent condition* as 或有的, *condition precedent* as 先決條件, and *condition subsequent* as 後決條件.

12. *Chitty* at para. 12-031 defines this term: 'In its most technical sense, however, it is to be understood as meaning a term of the contract, the breach of which may give rise to a claim for damages but not a right to treat the contract as repudiated. The use of the word "warranty" in this sense is reserved for the less important terms of a contract, or those which are collateral to the main purpose of the contract, the breach of which by one party does not entitle the other to treat his obligations as discharged.' See also *Butterworths* at 255 (discussing the Sale of Goods Ordinance (Cap 26) section 55).
13. 18 *Halsbury's* at para. 115.360.
14. *Chui and Roebuck* at para. 4.9.2. Another authority explains: 'Some contractual undertakings are too complex to be fitted into that scheme and the legal consequences of breach of such an undertaking . . . [depend] upon the effect of the breach. If the breach deprives the innocent party of substantially the whole benefit of the contract, or, in other words, if it goes so much to the root of the contract that it makes further commercial performance of the contract impossible, in addition to any remedy in damages the innocent party will be entitled to be discharged from further obligation; but if the event does not have that effect its consequences can be remedied only by an award of damages.' 18 *Halsbury's* at para. 115.362.
15. *Chitty* at para. 12-035. See also *Furmston* at 199–205; *Ho* at 246–250.
16. *Chitty* at para. 12-034.
17. As explained by 18 *Halsbury's* at para. 115.151:

> During the course of the formation of a contract, one of the persons who are to become parties to the contract may make representations to another such person. A representation is a statement made by one party (the representor) to another party (the representee) which relates, by way of affirmation, denial, description or otherwise, to a matter of fact or present intention.
>
> A representation of fact may or may not be intended to have contractual force; if it is so intended, it will amount to a contractual term; if it is not so intended, it is termed a mere representation.

The *BLIS Glossary* translates *representation* as 陳述.

18. 18 *Halsbury's* at para. 115.152. An example of the factors for determining intention is set out in id.
19. *Chui and Roebuck* at para. 4.3 notes: 'We have to allow for what is known as "trader's puff". . . . One rule of thumb is that when the remark concerns facts which can be checked, it is more likely to be a representation. So if a car

salesman says "this car has only had one owner", this cannot possibly be a mere puff, for a statement of fact is being made. If he says "this is a delightful little car", that sounds more like a puff.'

20. *Fisher and Greenwood* at 221.

21. In *Bannerman v White* (1861) 9 WR 784, the defendant intended to purchase grain from the plaintiff. During the negotiations, the defendant stated that he would not purchase any grain grown using sulphur. The plaintiff stated that no sulphur had been used in the cultivation. In fact, sulphur was used in growing the grain. The parties then entered into the contract for the sale and purchase of the grain. The court held that the plaintiff's assurance amounted to a term of the contract.

22. See Chapter 7, section A and section C for discussion on *damages* and *specific performance* respectively. *Specific performance* is defined as an equitable remedy whereby a court orders a party to a contract to specifically perform its obligations under the contract. *Black's Law Dictionary* at 1297 defines *equitable remedy* as 'a nonmonetary remedy, such as an injunction or specific performance, obtained when monetary damages cannot adequately redress the injury'.

    Id. at 560 defines *equity* as:

    (1) Fairness; impartiality; even-handed dealing.
    (2) The body of principles constituting what is fair and right; natural law.
    (3) The recourse to principles of justice to correct or supplement the law as applied to particular circumstances.
    (4) The system of law or body of principles originating in the English Court of Chancery and superseding the common and statute law when the two conflict.

    As noted by *Fisher and Greenwood* at 13: 'The maxims of equity still direct the courts in the exercise of their discretion whether or not to grant equitable relief. The principle that "he who comes to equity must come with clean hands" means that equitable remedies or "relief" will only be granted to those who have acted fairly in respect of the contract. The principle that "he who seeks equity must do equity" means that equitable relief will be granted only where the claimant is prepared to comply with the requirements of the court to do justice to the other party.'

    The *BLIS Glossary* translates *equity* as 衡平法 and *equitable remedy* as 衡平法補救. *Equitable relief* may be translated as 衡平法濟助.

23. *Chui and Roebuck* at para. 4.7.2.9. For cases involving the issue of interpretation of contract, see, e.g., *Jumbo King Ltd v Faithful Properties Ltd* (1999) 2 HKCFAR 279; *Konwall Construction & Engineering Co Ltd v Strong Progress Ltd* [2013] 3 HKLRD 503; *Paul's Model Art GmbH v UT Ltd* [2013] HKEC 1397.

24. *Chitty* at paras. 12-043–12-044 (emphasis in original). As for the general rules of construction or interpretation used by the courts, see id. at paras. 12-045–12-133; the cases cited in the previous note and in note 1.

25. Krishnan Arjunan and Abdul Majid bin Nabi Baksh, *Business Law in Hong Kong* (2nd edition, 2009) [hereinafter *Arjunan and Nabi Baksh*] translates *contra proferentem* as 不利於提出合約的一方.

26. *Chui and Roebuck* at para. 4.7. In *Tam Wing Chuen v Bank of Credit and Commerce Hong Kong Ltd* [1996] 2 BCLC 69, 77, the court commented on *contra proferentem* by saying: 'a person who puts forward the wording of a proposed agreement may be assumed to have looked after his own interest so that if the words leave room for doubt about whether he is intended to have a particular benefit there is reason to suppose that he is not.'

27. 18 *Halsbury's* at para. 115.363 explains: 'There will be a fundamental breach . . . entitling the innocent party to be discharged, if the breach has produced a situation fundamentally different from anything which the parties could, as reasonable men, have contemplated when the contract was made. . . . a fundamental term is no more than a condition, that is a term which the parties have agreed either expressly or impliedly which goes to the root of the contract, so that any breach of that term . . . will allow the innocent party to treat himself as discharged.'

    Chitty at para. 12-021 describes *fundamental term* as being an essential part of the agreement: 'The fundamental term has been described as part of the "core" of the contract, the non-performance of which destroys the very substance of the agreement. . . . Examples usually cited are those where a seller delivers goods wholly different from the agreed contract goods or delivers goods which are so seriously defective as to render them in substance not the goods contracted for: e.g. the delivery of beans instead of peas, of pinewood logs instead of mahogany logs, or of a vehicle which is incapable or barely capable of self-propulsion instead of a motor car. In each case, so it is said, there is a breach of the fundamental term, that is to say, of the "core" obligation to deliver the essential goods which are the subject-matter of the contract of sale.'

28. *Chui and Roebuck* at para. 4.9.2. See *Butterworths* at 102–5.

29. *Cehave NV v Bremer Handelsgesellschaft mbH (The Hansa Nord)* [1976] 1 QB 44, 61.

30. The *BLIS Glossary* translates *exclusion clause* as 免責條款. *LexisNexis, Hong Kong English-Chinese Legal Dictionary 718 (2005)* [hereinafter *LexisNexis*] translates *exemption clause* and *limitation clause* as 免責條款 and 限制條款 respectively.

31. *Chui and Roebuck* at para. 8.4.

32. The *BLIS Glossary* translates *public policy* as 公共政策. For a more detailed explanation in interpreting an exemption clause, see *Lewison* at 574–78.

33. See *Lewison* at 586–89 for a discussion of ambiguous exemption clauses and id. at 609–15 for a discussion of courts' interpretation of exemption clauses.

34. 18 *Halsbury's* at para. 115.174 provides in detail:

For an exclusion clause to be incorporated into a contract, the party against whom it is to operate must be given reasonable notice of its existence. Whether such notice has been given is determined according to the following principles:

(1) If the party against whom the clause operates has actual knowledge of the clause at the time when the contract is concluded he is inevitably bound by it.

(2) When there is no actual knowledge, the party against whom the clause operates will not be bound if he has no reason to believe that the document containing the clause contained contractual terms.

(3) If the party against whom the clause operates has reason to believe that a document given to him contains contractual terms he may be bound by those terms, including any exclusion clause, even though he does not choose to read the document; if the document contains what is reasonably necessary to bring the terms to the attention of a reader, the recipient will be bound, but he will not be bound if it does not do so.

(4) If the party putting forward the exclusion clause in his favour (the proferens) has done that which is normally sufficient to give reasonable notice of the clause, it may bind the other party even though, due to some personal disability, he is unable to understand the clause. It may be, however, that if such disability is known to the party seeking to impose the exclusion clause he must take such further steps as are reasonable to bring the clause to the notice of the person under the disability.

(5) Where the exclusion clause upon which a party seeks to rely is printed only in English or only in Chinese and the other party cannot read that language, it is necessary to ask the further question: Has the party relying on the unsigned term done all that could be reasonably required of him to draw the other party's attention to the existence of terms in the document in such a way that the other party cannot be heard to say that he did not read them?

(6) It may be that the more onerous the consequences of the exclusion clause for the party on whom it is imposed, the more forceful must be the notice which he is given of it.

(7) In the absence of fraud or misrepresentation a party will be bound by an exclusion clause in a document which he has signed, provided at least that the document appeared to be of a contractual nature and that the term was capable of exclusion.

(8) If the effect of an exclusion clause is misrepresented by the party seeking to impose it, or by his agent, he will be held to the meaning of the clause as represented; and a similar principle applies where that party or his agent gives a collateral assurance that varies or extinguishes the effect of the exclusion clause.

35. *Thornton v Shoe Lane Parking Ltd* [1971] 2 QB 163, 169.
36. 18 *Halsbury's* at para. 115.174.
37. *Ying Wei (Hop Yick) Cargo Service v Nanyang Credit Card Co Ltd* [1993] 1 HKC 56, 59.
38. For a summary of the provisions in this ordinance, see *Butterworths* at 272–73.
39. 18 *Halsbury's* at para. 115.194; *Lewison* at 468–69. See section 8 of the Control of Exemption Clauses Ordinance (Cap 71).
40. Schedule 1 of the Control of Exemption Clauses Ordinance.
41. See, e.g., section 3 of the Control of Exemption Clauses Ordinance which provides in relevant part:

(1) . . . the requirement of reasonableness for the purposes of this Ordinance and section 4 of the Misrepresentation Ordinance (Cap 284) is satisfied only if the court . . . determines that the term was a fair and reasonable one . . . having regard to the circumstances which were, or ought reasonably to have been, known to or in the contemplation of the parties when the contract was made.

(2) In determining . . . whether a contract term satisfies the requirement of reasonableness, the court . . . shall have regard in particular to the matters specified in Schedule 2; but this subsection does not prevent the court . . . from holding, in accordance with any rule of law, that a term which purports to exclude or restrict any relevant liability is not a term of the contract.

(3) In relation to a notice (not being a notice having contractual effect), the requirement of reasonableness under this Ordinance is satisfied only if the court . . . determines that it would be fair and reasonable to allow reliance on it, having regard to all the circumstances obtaining when the liability arose or (but for the notice) would have arisen.

(4) In determining (under this Ordinance or the Misrepresentation Ordinance (Cap 284)) whether a contract term or notice satisfies the requirement of reasonableness, the court . . . shall have regard in particular . . . to whether . . . the language in which the term or notice is expressed is a language understood by the person as against whom another person seeks to rely upon the term or notice.

(5) Where by reference to a contract term or notice a person seeks to restrict liability to a specified sum of money, and the question arises (under this Ordinance or the Misrepresentation Ordinance (Cap 284)) whether the term or notice satisfies the requirement of reasonableness, the court . . . shall have regard in particular (but without prejudice to subsection (2) or (4)) to–
    (a) the resources which he could expect to be available to him for the purpose of meeting the liability should it arise; and
    (b) how far it was open to him to cover himself by insurance.

See also Schedule 2 of the Control of Exemption Clauses Ordinance which provides additional guidelines for determining *reasonableness*:

(a) the strength of the bargaining positions of the parties relative to each other, taking into account (among other things) alternative means by which the customer's requirements could have been met;
(b) whether the customer received an inducement to agree to the term, or in accepting it had an opportunity of entering into a similar contract with other persons, but without having to accept a similar term;
(c) whether the customer knew or ought reasonably to have known of the existence and extent of the term (having regard, among other things, to any custom of the trade and any previous course of dealing between the parties);
(d) where the term excludes or restricts any relevant liability if some condition is not complied with, whether it was reasonable at the time of the contract to expect that compliance with that condition would be practicable;
(e) whether the goods were manufactured, processed or adapted to the special order of the customer.

42. 18 *Halsbury's* at para. 115.204.

43. *David Friedman v Sieger Ltd* [2014] HKEC 44, para. 20. See also cases cited in the notes in section A of this chapter; *Lewison* at Chapter 8 ('Ambiguity and Uncertainty').

Chapter 5

1. Note the differences between a *void* contract, a *voidable* contract and an *unenforceable* contract. A void contract has no legal effect. Strictly speaking, no contract has ever come into existence at all. For example, at common law, a contract formed by mistake is void. A voidable contract is a valid agreement until any party thereto raises a vitiating factor (see the discussion in this section on vitiating factors) and wants to avoid it. A contract involving misrepresentation is an example of a voidable contract. An unenforceable contract is a valid contract but because of some reason the parties cannot enforce

the contractual rights/duties through a court, e.g., contract (not for necessity) with a minor or oral contract for sale of land. *Ho* at 285–86. The *BLIS Glossary* translates *void* as 無效, *voidable* as 可使無效, and *unenforceable* as 不能強制執行.

2. 18 *Halsbury's* at para. 115.030 notes: 'In general, a valid contract may be made by any person recognised by law as having legal personality, that is natural persons, corporations and the Hong Kong Special Administrative Region. However, the following classes of persons are in law incompetent to contract, or are only capable of contracting to a limited extent or in a particular manner: (1) bankrupts; (2) minors; (3) persons of unsound mind; (4) alien enemies; (5) drunkards; (6) corporations; (7) companies; (8) partnerships; and (9) receivers of companies.'

3. See Interpretation and General Clauses Ordinance (Cap 1) section 3, which states in part: '"adult" (成人、成年人) means a person who has attained the age of 18 years'. See also Age of Majority (Related Provisions) Ordinance (Cap 410) section 2, which states in part:

   (1) . . . a person shall attain full age on attaining the age of 18 years.
   (2) A person who, on the date of commencement of this Ordinance, has already attained the age of 18 years but not the age of 21 years, shall attain full age on that date.

4. See Mental Health Ordinance (Cap 136) section 2 which provides, in part, definitions for the following conditions:

   "mental disorder" (精神紊亂)
   "mentally disordered" (精神紊亂)
   "mental handicap" (弱智)
   "mental incapacity" (精神上無行為能力)
   "mentally disordered person" (精神紊亂的人)
   "mentally handicapped person" (弱智人士)
   "mentally incapacitated person" (精神上無行為能力的人)
   "psychopathic disorder" (精神病理障礙)
   "sub-average general intellectual functioning" (低於平均的一般智能)

5. Section 46 of the District Court Ordinance (Cap 336) states:

   No person shall by reason of his not having attained the full age . . . be exempted from liability for any debt, damages or demand arising under an agreement made before the date of commencement of the Age of Majority (Related Provisions) Ordinance (Cap 410) where the debt, damages or demand–

   (a) does not exceed the sum of $60000; or
   (b) has been reduced to a sum not exceeding $60000 by reason of the plaintiff having abandoned the amount in excess of $60000 in his cause of action.

   See also Age of Majority (Related Provisions) Ordinance (Cap 410) section 4.

6. *Chui and Roebuck* at para. 11.3.3. See also *Chitty* at paras 8-001–8-068.
7. See, e.g., Companies Ordinance (Cap 622) section 115 to section 120, which provides: requirements with respect to memorandum, powers of a company, power limited by memorandum, etc., and exclusion of deemed notice.
8. A recent Hong Kong case has reviewed some of the items which we will be addressing in this section. In *Midland Realty (Comm & Ind) Ltd v NCF (HK) Ltd* [2015] HKEC 905, the court stated:

> 62. Where one person makes a false representation to another with the object and result of inducing the representee to enter into a contract with him or her, the representee is generally entitled to rescind the contract.
>
> 63. Statements concerning the object or effect of a document or words in documents are statements of fact and, as such, are representations.
>
> 64. Statements concerning private rights, as distinct from the general law, are statements of fact.
>
> 65. The question is whether a person was induced by the representation and it is a question of fact to be asked in respect of the particular representee, as opposed to an objective reasonable bystander.
>
> 66. If a representation is such that it was likely that a person in the representee's position would rely on it, a court may find it easier to believe the representee's assertion that he did rely on it. The materiality of the statement is evidence that goes towards establishing reliance.
>
> 67. A misrepresentation is material if it is something that induces the person to whom it is made to contract on the terms on which he does contract . . . If a man has a material misstatement made to him which may, from its nature, induce him to enter into the contract, it is an inference that he was induced by it to enter into the contract.
>
> 68. The representation need not be the sole or predominant cause of entering into the contract. As long as any one of the representee's motives for entering into the contract is vitiated by the misinformation given by the other party, it is enough to undermine the whole transaction. (citations omitted)

For in-depth analysis of this topic, see *Chitty* at paras. 6-001–6-044; 6-099–6-107. See also *Butterworths* at 106–9.

9. See the case of *Edgington v Fitzmaurice* (1885) 29 Ch D 459. *Furmston* at 340 defines misrepresentation as follows: 'A representation is a statement of fact made by one party to the contract (the representor) to the other (the representee) which, [while not part] of the contract, is yet one of the reasons that induces the representee to enter into the contract. A misrepresentation is simply a representation that is untrue. The representor's state of mind and

degree of carefulness are not relevant to classifying a representation as a misrepresentation but only to determining the type of misrepresentation.'

The *BLIS Glossary* translates *innocent misrepresentation* as 無意的失實陳述, *fraudulent or reckless misrepresentation* as 有欺詐成分或罔顧後果的失實陳述, and *negligent misrepresentation* as 疏忽的失實陳述.

10. *Fisher and Greenwood* at 213.

11. Id.

12. *Chui and Roebuck* at para. 5.2.1.

13. *LexisNexis* translates *uberrimae fidei* as 完全坦率真誠.

14. *Smith v Land and House Property Corp* (1884) LR 28 Ch D 7, 12.

15. *Chitty* at para. 6-012; *Ho* at 294–95. As stated by the court in the case of *Kwok Wing Kiu v Boxing Promotions Ltd* [2013] HKEC 798: 'It is trite that if a person is prevented from following a future intended course of action or simply changes his mind, this will not render the statement as to his original intention a misrepresentation.' Id. at para. 25 (citations omitted).

16. *Rescission* is the right allowed in equity to the innocent party to cancel the contract, if it so chooses. If the injured party selects this choice, the contract is rescinded and the parties are placed back into their pre-contract positions.

    18 *Halsbury's* at para. 115.353 defines the terms as follows: 'Rescission is the name given to a process whereby an existing contract is brought to an end and the effects of its existence are cancelled or terminated . . . it seems that where rescission is sought on equitable grounds its effect is to restore the parties to the position before the contract was entered into, whereas rescission at common law for breach simply discharges the parties from further obligations to perform the contract.'

17. *Ho* at 290 notes the term *innocent misrepresentation* should refer to misrepresentation made without fraud and without negligence. *Chitty* at paras. 6-005 and 6-099 defines the term *innocent misrepresentation* as a representation which is neither fraudulent nor negligent.

18. 44 *Halsbury's* at paras. 340.011–340.015.

19. See, e.g., *Chitty* at para. 6-099, explaining: 'The term "innocent misrepresentation" is here used to mean a representation which is neither fraudulent nor negligent, and the general rule remains . . . that no action for damages lies for a mere innocent misrepresentation . . . a misrepresentation will found a claim for damages if it can be construed as a contractual promise, and is either part of a wider contract, or is itself supported by consideration. This may happen in two principal types of case. First, where the representor and representee themselves enter into a contract after the misrepresentation was made. Here, if the misrepresentation becomes a term of the contract, an action for damages will lie, whether the misrepresentation was fraudulent, negligent or innocent. Secondly, the representee may enter into a contract with a third party as a result of the misrepresentation. Even in this situation, it is often possible to construe the misrepresentation as a collateral contract, the consideration for

which is supplied by the fact that the representee enters into the contract with the third party.'

20. What constitutes *too much time* depends upon the circumstances, according to the court in the case of *Leaf v International Galleries* [1950] 2 KB 86. See also 18 *Halsbury's* at para. 115.479. The *BLIS Glossary* translates *equitable doctrine* as 衡平法則 and *laches* as 就行使權利方面的疏忽延誤.
21. Section 2 of the Misrepresentation Ordinance (Cap 284) provides:

> Where a person has entered into a contract after a misrepresentation has been made to him, and–
> (a) the misrepresentation has become a term of the contract; or
> (b) the contract has been performed,
> or both, then, if otherwise he would be entitled to rescind the contract without alleging fraud, he shall be so entitled, subject to the provisions of this Ordinance, notwithstanding the matters mentioned in paragraphs (a) and (b).

22. The *BLIS Glossary* translates this term as 付出價值的真誠購買人 and provides this alternative translation of *bona fide purchaser* as 真誠買方.
23. For an in-depth analysis of this topic, see *Chitty* at paras. 6-001–6-044; 6-046–6-071.
24. *Derry v Peek* (1889) 14 App Cas 337, 374. *Ho* at 288 states: 'A fraudulent misrepresentation then is one made without honest belief in its truth. This dishonesty can be proved by showing that the representor knew of the falsity of his representation, or that he shut his eyes to the facts or deliberately abstained from inquiry into them. This formulation suggests some moral blameworthiness, but it is not necessary to prove moral blame.'
25. *Chitty* at para. 6-047, and also notes at paras. 6-049–6-050. In order to establish fraudulent misrepresentation, the plaintiff needs to show the defendant's lack of an honest belief. *Chitty* states at paras. 6-049–6-050:

> The requirement of proof of the absence of honest belief does not, however, mean that the claimant must prove the defendant's knowledge of the falsity of the statement. It is enough to establish that the latter suspected that his statement might be inaccurate, or that he neglected to inquire into its accuracy, without proving that he actually knew that it was false.
>
> Further, it is not necessary to establish that the defendant's motive was dishonest.

26. Id. at para. 6-047.
27. The *BLIS Glossary* translates *avoid* as 廢止.
28. *Fisher and Greenwood* at 234 (emphasis in original).
29. For an in-depth analysis, see *Chitty* at paras. 6-001–6-044; 6-046–6-098.

30. *Butterworths* at 110 refers to *negligent misrepresentation* as: 'A misrepresentation is innocent if there is honest belief in its truth, which becomes negligent misrepresentation if the representor had no reasonable grounds to believe in its truth. A negligent misrepresentation results from want of care, skill or competence or lapse of memory, whereas a fraudulent misrepresentation results from dishonesty.'

31. *Stone* at 315. For another analysis of *mistake*, see Clemence Yeung, *The Law of Unjust Enrichment in Hong Kong* (2008) 217–57 [hereinafter *Yeung*].

32. *Stone* at 312.

33. *Fisher and Greenwood* at 245.

34. *Chui and Roebuck* at para. 5.4.

35. Id.

36. *Fisher and Greenwood* at 245. If a mistake is *operative*, it is sufficiently serious to justify court intervention. *Stone* at 315n15.

37. The *BLIS Glossary* translates *ab initio* as 一開始 and *Arjunan and Nabi Baksh* at *liii* translates *ab initio* as 由最初開始 respectively. As for the consequences of payments made under this situation, see, e.g., Andrew Burrows, *A Restatement of The English Law of Unjust Enrichment* (2012) 9–10 [hereinafter *Burrows*].

38. See *Ho* at 379–87; 44 *Halsbury's* at paras. 340.006–340.010. *LexisNexis* translates *rectification* as 糾正. The *BLIS Glossary* translates *rectify* as 更正.

39. *Chui and Roebuck* at para. 5.5. Rectification is: 'where a contract has by reason of a mistake common to the contracting parties been drawn up so as to [be contrary to] . . . the terms intended by both as revealed in their previous oral understanding, the court will rectify the document so as to carry out such intentions. . . . Rectification will not be ordered . . . [if] a written agreement fails to mention a matter because the parties simply overlooked it, having no intention on the point at all, nor if they decided deliberately to omit the issue. In such cases the written agreement must be construed as it stands.' *Chitty* at para. 5-111.

40. *Codelfa Construction Proprietary Ltd v State Rail Authority of NSW* (1982) 149 CLR 337, 346. For a discussion of the difference between correction of an error and the rectification of a contract, see *Lewison* at 468–69.

41. As for a mistake of fact: 'It has long been clear that money paid under a mistake of the payer as to a material fact is, in certain circumstances, recoverable. Mistake in this context means lack of knowledge of the absence of liability, but it is notoriously difficult to make an authoritative statement of the principles upon which recovery is based.' *Chitty* at para. 29-030.

As for a mistake of law, id. at para. 29-041 states: 'Despite a dubious legal foundation and the difficulty of drawing any clear dividing line between "law" and "fact", for many years as a general rule money paid under a mistake as to the general law, or as to the legal effect of the circumstances under which it is paid, but with full knowledge of the facts, was irrecoverable.'

Traditionally, payments made under mistake of law (as opposed to mistake of fact) were not recoverable. However, this general rule that mistake of fact is operative while mistake of law is inoperative is no longer followed in the United Kingdom. Several cases have recently abolished this distinction: *Kleinwort Benson Ltd v Lincoln City Council* [1999] 2 AC 349 (discussed in *Chitty* at paras. 29-045–29-046); *Pankhania v The London Borough of Hackney* [2002] EWHC 2441 (Ch); *Brennan v Bolt Burdon* [2004] 1 WLR 1240 (QB).

The *Brennan* court noted that:

> at common law a mistake of law did not vitiate a contract. A mistake of fact in some circumstances could vitiate the contract. The difficulty was in distinguishing between a mistake of law and a mistake of fact. In order to grant relief "mistakes of law" were sometimes described as "mistakes of fact" ([2004] 1 WLR 1251, para. 45)
>
> . . .
>
> In my judgment the courts should be very slow to set aside and declare compromise agreements void on the ground of alleged common mistakes of fact or law. Before declaring a compromise agreement void the court must be satisfied that the mistake, in this case of law, was both common and fundamental to the making of the compromise agreement . . . (id. at 1252, para. 50)

Hong Kong has also eliminated the distinction between mistake in fact and mistake in law in relation to payments. See 18 *Halsbury's* at para. 115. 443. The *BLIS Glossary* translates *mistake of fact* as 事實方面的錯誤 and *LexisNexis* translates *mistake of law* as 法律錯誤.

42. *Chui and Roebuck* at para. 5.4.3 defines this term as where: 'one party only has made a mistake, but a mistake of which the other knows or, on an objective test, ought to know'.

Chitty at para. 5-067 has noted: 'No contract can be formed if there is no correspondence between the offer and the acceptance, or if the agreement is not sufficiently certain. . . . If, however, one party claims that he did not intend to contract at all, or did not intend to contract on the terms which the other party claims were agreed, then the question is whether, there is a contract (or, as it is often put, whether or not the "contract is void"). The intention of the parties is, as a general rule, to be construed objectively.'

For further detailed discussions, see *Fisher and Greenwood* at 248; *Butterworths* at 114–19.

43. *Chui and Roebuck* at para. 5.4.3. For other examples of successful claims of unilateral mistake, see, e.g., *Hartog v Colin and Shields* [1939] 3 All ER 566. (The seller mistakenly quoted the selling price as per pound rather than per piece. The buyer accepted the lower per pound price. The court held that the buyer could not claim a contract as the parties had negotiated the price on the per piece basis which was the trade standard and the buyer should have known of the mistake.) Or, see *Chwee Kin Keong v Digilandmall.com Pte Ltd* [2005] 1 SLR 502. (The seller mistakenly listed $3,900 product for sale at $66;

the buyer claimed not to know of this mistake. The court found, based upon the number of orders placed and the time of placing the orders, the buyer had knowledge of the mistake.)

44. 18 *Halsbury's* at para. 115.102 explains: 'A mistake as to the terms of the offer must be carefully distinguished from a mistake as to the quality of what is being offered. A mistake as to the terms which are being offered raises problems of offer and acceptance; but a mistake as to the quality of what is being offered usually does not. . . . it is well-established that a mistaken motive of one party cannot prevent the formation of an agreement, even if realised by the other party.'

45. *Furmston* at 294 provides that: 'In common mistake, both parties make the same mistake. Each knows the intention of the other and accepts it, but each is mistaken about some underlying and fundamental fact. The parties, for example, are unaware that the subject matter of their contract has already perished.'

    Fisher and Greenwood at 248 states that: 'Common mistake arises when the parties are in agreement, but that agreement assumes some fact to be true when it is not.'

    For additional detailed discussions, see *Chui and Roebuck* at para. 5.4.1; *Butterworths* at 113, 116–17.

46. Along similar, but not identical, lines to the consequences of common mistake is section 8 of the Sale of Goods Ordinance (Cap 26) which provides that: 'Where there is a contract for the sale of specific goods, and the goods, without the knowledge of the seller, have perished at the time when the contract is made, the contract is void.'

47. *Great Peace Shipping Ltd v Tsavliris (International) Ltd* [2003] QB 679, 703 (para. 76).

48. *Bell v Lever Bros* [1932] AC 161, 218.

49. Id. at 224.

50. The impact of this case upon Hong Kong is unclear although there is a suggestion that Hong Kong courts would follow this narrowing of the application of common mistake. *Fisher and Greenwood* at 246, 254–58. See also *Chitty* at paras. 5-036, 5-060–5-061 for a discussion of this case, and id. at paras. 5-057–5-063 for a discussion of the impact of this case upon the application of equity to common mistake.

51. There is divergence among the authorities as to the terminology. *Chitty* at para. 5-001, note 3 states: 'earlier editions of this work used the phrase "mutual mistake", following the terminology used by Lord Atkin in *Bell v Lever Bros* [1932] A.C. 161, and until recently some other works adhered to this usage . . . It is now more common to refer to this type of mistake as "common mistake" . . . One reason for using the phrase "common mistake" is to reduce the risk of confusion with what is termed here "mutual

misunderstanding" (where the parties are at cross-purposes as to the terms of the contract).'

Furmston at 294 states: 'In mutual mistake, the parties misunderstand each other and are at cross-purposes. A, for example, intends to offer his Toyota Prius car for sale, but B believes that the offer relates to the Toyota Aventis also owned by A.'

Fisher and Greenwood at 248 explains: 'Mutual mistake arises when the parties are at cross purposes; each misunderstanding the other.'

See *Butterworths* at 113–14.

52. *Chui and Roebuck* at para. 5.4.2.

53. *Furmston* at 294–95 notes in regard to mutual and unilateral mistakes:

> Where either mutual or unilateral mistake is pleaded, the very existence of the agreement is denied. The argument is that, despite appearances, there is no real correspondence of offer and acceptance and that therefore the transaction must necessarily be void.
> . . . If mutual mistake is pleaded, the judicial approach . . . is objective; the court, looking at the evidence from the standpoint of a reasonable third party, will decide whether any, and if so what, agreement must be taken to have been reached. If unilateral mistake is pleaded, the approach is subjective; the innocent party is allowed to show the effect upon *his* mind of the error in the hope of avoiding its consequences. (emphasis in original)

Fisher and Greenwood at 249 comments that: 'Unilateral and mutual mistakes are instances where the mistake *negatives* consent; the parties never reach agreement.' (emphasis in original)

54. *Kowloon Development Finance Ltd v Pendex Industries Ltd* (2013) 16 HKCFAR 336 (CFA), 345–46.

55. *Arjunan and Nabi Baksh* at lxxi translates *non est factum* as 否定簽訂合約. For a more detailed discussion of *non est factum*, see *Butterworths* at 119–20.

56. *Saunders v Anglia Building Society* [1971] AC 1004, 1017.

57. *Lee Tit Fan v Strong Base International Industrial Ltd* [2012] HKEC 512, para. 33. See also *Wing Hang Credit Ltd v Hui Chun Kit Benjamin* [2011] HKEC 1447.

58. *Pathak Ravi Dutt v Sanjeev Maheshwari* [2014] 3 HKLRD 597, 605–6.

59. As Nelson Enonchong notes: 'two requirements which must be satisfied for relief to be available on the ground of duress. There must be pressure which amounts to compulsion of the will of the complainant and the pressure must be one which the law does not regard as legitimate'. See *Duress, Undue Influence and Unconscionable Dealing* para. 2-002 (2nd edition, 2012) (citation omitted) [hereinafter *Enonchong*]. This guidance has been cited with approval as the applicable law in Hong Kong by the court in *Lau Ying Wai v Emperor Regency International* [2015] HKEC 53.

60. *Chui and Roebuck* at para. 5.6.1. As noted in 18 *Halsbury's* at para. 115.104:

> By duress is meant the compulsion under which a person acts through fear of personal suffering as from injury to the body or from confinement, actual or threatened. . . . There is no duress simply because a party has to enter into a contract by reason of statutory compulsion, or the fact that the other party is a monopoly supplier. Moreover, as a general rule, a threat of civil proceedings or bankruptcy proceedings does not amount to duress, whether there is good foundation for the proceedings or not; but it may do so if it is intended and calculated . . . to cause terror in the particular case. The question whether imprisonment or threatened imprisonment does or does not constitute duress depends upon whether the imprisonment is lawful or unlawful.
>
> . . .
>
> A contract obtained by means of duress exercised by one party over the other is at very least voidable, and may perhaps be void; but if it is voluntarily acted upon by the party entitled to avoid, it will become binding on him. The duress must be actually existing at the time of the making of the contract; and the personal suffering . . . may be that of the husband or wife or near relative of the contracting party, but that of a stranger or a master is not sufficient.

See also *Butterworths* at 120–21, 124; *Yeung* at Chapter 9 ('Duress').

61. The concept of economic duress: 'amounts to recognising that certain threats or forms of pressure, not associated with threats to the person, nor limited to the seizure or withholding of goods, may give grounds for relief to a party who enters into a contract as a result of the threats or the pressure'. *Chitty* at para. 7-015.

Fisher and Greenwood at 277 explains: 'Economic duress occurs where some unfair and unlawful economic pressure is placed on a party to a contract. While it may sometimes be difficult to distinguish between duress and legitimate, hard bargaining, the key elements of economic duress are "illegitimate pressure" and lack of a practical alternative.'

See *Butterworths* at 121–24.

62. *Occidental Worldwide Investment Corporation v Skibs AS/Avanti (The Sibeon v The Sibotre)* [1976] 1 Lloyd's Rep 293.

63. *Chui and Roebuck* at para. 5.6.2. These authors explain economic duress through a review of the following case:

> For example, in *North Ocean Shipping v. Hyundai Construction: The Atlantic Baron* [1979] QB 705, the builders of a ship were to be paid in US dollars. At the time the dollar was dropping, they told the buyers that unless they increased the payment by 10%, there would be no delivery on the due date. The builders knew that the buyers had many commitments and needed the ship. The court was satisfied that there was economic duress. The renegotiation was prompted

> by coercion by the builders, who twisted circumstances under their power. This is why most cases have so far been about renegotiations—because there it is clear that it is not merely market forces which are involved. As it happens, the buyers still lost their case. They paid a final instalment after delivery, and this was held to be affirmation after duress had ceased. (Id.)

64. *Atlas Express Ltd v Kafco Ltd* [1989] QB 833; *Chitty* at paras. 7-032–7-037. See also *Ho* at 407–14. As for the consequences of payments made under this situation, see *Burrows* at 10–11.
65. *Esquire (Electronics) Ltd v Hong Kong and Shanghai Banking Corp Ltd* [2007] 3 HKLRD 439 (CA), 492.
66. *Lau Ying Wai v Emperor Regency International* [2015] HKEC 53, para. 13.
67. One source states that the doctrine of undue influence is equity's version of the common law's doctrine of duress. Undue influence relates to those circumstances where pressure of a more subtle nature than recognised by the doctrine of duress has been used to persuade a party to enter into a contract. *Fisher and Greenwood* at 277. See 44 *Halsbury's* at para. 340.150; *Chitty* at paras. 7-057–7-143; *Butterworths* at 125. The *BLIS Glossary* translates *unconscionable* as 不合情理 and *acted unconscionably* as 作出不合情理的作為.
68. The *BLIS Glossary* translates *undue influence* as 不當影響 and *equitable doctrine* as 衡平法則.
69. *Chitty* at para. 7-101 notes: 'A transaction entered into as the result of undue influence is voidable and not void. The right to rescind on the ground of undue influence may be lost either by express affirmation of the transaction by the victim, by estoppel or by delay amounting to proof of acquiescence. . . . to be of any value, the affirmation must take place after the influence has ceased . . . Lapse of time in itself does not seem to constitute a bar to relief, but it will provide evidence of acquiescence if the victim fails to take any steps to set aside the transaction within a reasonable time after he is freed from the undue influence.'
70. 18 *Halsbury's* at para. 115.106 states in part:

> Undue influence may be defined . . . as the unconscientious use by one person of power possessed by him over another in order to induce the other to enter into a contract. It will be established where the party seeking to set the transaction aside establishes four things: (1) the other party or another who induced the transaction had the capacity to influence the first party; (2) that influence was exercised; (3) the exercise of influence was undue; and (4) the exercise of influence induced the transaction.
>
> . . . the existence of a relationship of presumed special trust and confidence between the contracting parties (such as that of parent and child, guardian and ward, trustee and beneficiary, solicitor and client, doctor and patient, or priest and confessor, but not husband

and wife) merely relieves the dependent party of the obligation to prove that he reposed special trust and confidence in the other party in relation to the impugned contractual transaction: There arises, instead, an irrebuttable presumption that such trust and confidence existed in relation to the conclusion of that transaction. It does not follow from the existence of a presumed relationship of special trust and confidence, however, that the impugned transaction was induced by undue influence. More is needed than the presumed relationship of special trust and confidence. In particular, the dependent party must show that the transaction inflicted on him 'a transaction which calls for explanation'. Where the relationship of special trust exists (either because it arises from a type of relationship in which such trust and confidence is irrebuttably presumed, or where in other situations it has been independently proven on the balance of probabilities) and the dependent party can point to a 'transaction which calls for explanation', then a court is entitled to infer that 'in the absence of a satisfactory explanation the transaction can only have been procured by undue influence'.

It is not permissible to infer merely from the fact that a transaction is manifestly disadvantageous to a party that he has entered into it as a result of undue influence.

71. For a discussion of these relationships, see, e.g., *Fisher and Greenwood* at 293–311; *Ho* at 418–26; *Chitty* at paras. 7-073–7-129; *Furmston* at 398–408; *Enonchong* at Chapter 14 ('Abuse of Confidence'). The *BLIS Glossary* translates *fiduciary relationship* as 受信關係. As for the consequences of payments made under this situation, see *Burrows* at 11–12; *Yeung* at Chapter 10 ('Undue Influence').

72. *Enonchong* at Part IV—Third Party Duress, Undue Influence or Unconscionable Dealing.

73. 18 *Halsbury's* at para. 115.106 states in part: 'A court should not be too quick to find either that a wife reposed special trust or confidence in her husband (in the sense that she entrusted him with management of her financial affairs) or that a transaction that turned out to be disadvantageous to her was one calling for explanation. Although a husband is not presumed to exercise special influence over his wife, the reality is that a married couple's interests are intertwined in ways that those of, say, solicitor and client or medical advisor and patient are not. The Court of Appeal has observed that courts in Hong Kong will exercise a similar reticence concerning transactions among close family members more generally.'

74. *Diners Club International v Ng Chi-sing*, unreported, (1986) CA 143/85, 72, affirmed on appeal [1986] HKEC 113 (CA).

75. *Chui and Roebuck* at para. 5.7. This term is identically defined both in section 2 of the Securities and Futures (Client Securities) Rules (Cap 571H) and in section 2 of the Securities and Futures (Client Money) Rules (Cap 571I):

'"unconscionable" (不合情理), in relation to a standing authority, means unconscionable having regard to the factors specified in section 6 of the Unconscionable Contracts Ordinance (Cap 458), as if the standing authority in question were a contract under that Ordinance.'

Section 6(1) of the Unconscionable Contracts Ordinance (Cap 458) provides the criteria for finding an unconscionable agreement:

> In determining whether a contract or part of a contract was unconscionable in the circumstances relating to the contract at the time it was made, the court may have regard to (among other things)–
> (a) the relative strengths of the bargaining positions of the consumer and the other party;
> (b) whether, as a result of conduct engaged in by the other party, the consumer was required to comply with conditions that were not reasonably necessary for the protection of the legitimate interests of the other party;
> (c) whether the consumer was able to understand any documents relating to the supply or possible supply of the goods or services;
> (d) whether any undue influence or pressure was exerted on, or any unfair tactics were used against, the consumer or a person acting on behalf of the consumer by the other party or a person acting on behalf of the other party in relation to the supply or possible supply of the goods or services; and
> (e) the amount for which, and the circumstances under which, the consumer could have acquired identical or equivalent goods or services from a person other than the other party.

See also *Butterworths* at 125–26; *Enonchong* at paras. 15-003–15-004.

76. *Chitty* at para. 7-133. For further explanation on the topic of 'unconscionable bargains', see *Burrows* at 79–82, and *Yeung* at Chapter 11 ('Unconscionability').

77. 44 *Halsbury's* at para. 340.151. *Chow Ki Chuen v Choi Lin Fung Ada* [2014] HKEC 200, para. 64 applied these three indicia.

78. *LZX and WYL* [2012] 5 HKLRD 29, 44–45 (citations omitted).

79. *Tong Kwok Cheong and Tong Wai Lin* [2014] 1 HKLRD 339 (CA), 351–52 (citation omitted).

80. Section 5(1) of the Unconscionable Contracts Ordinance provides:

> If, with respect to a contract . . . in which one of the parties deals as consumer, the court finds the contract or any part of the contract to have been unconscionable in the circumstances relating to the contract at the time it was made, the court may–
> (a) refuse to enforce the contract;
> (b) enforce the remainder of the contract without the unconscionable part;

(c) limit the application of, or revise or alter, any unconscionable part so as to avoid any unconscionable result.

Section 6(1) of the of the Unconscionable Contracts Ordinance sets out the parameters to be considered by the courts in a claim of an unconscionable contract. Section 6(1) is set out in note 75. These two ordinances have been discussed in relation to exclusion clauses in Chapter 4, section C.

81. 18 *Halsbury's* at para. 115.207.

82. Id. at para. 115.246: 'The general rule is that a contract involving the commission of a legal wrong or a contract with an unlawful purpose may be not enforced by either party at law or in equity.'

Id. at para. 115.210: 'An agreement to do that which is a crime or a tort is illegal and will not be enforced by the courts.'

> Judges, in deciding the outcome of illegality cases, often draw a distinction between contracts which are illegal as *formed* and those illegal as *performed*. Thus, for example, a contract to jointly to rob a bank and then divide the proceeds is obviously illegal as formed. On the other hand a contract under which A agrees to ship B's goods is not, on the face of it, illegal but may be performed illegally if A decides to overload the ship contrary to law.
>
> Generally, when contracts are illegal as formed, the courts refuse to allow enforcement by either party. However, they may allow limited enforcement of an illegally formed contract via the "severance" of the part that is illegal.
>
> When, however, the contract is illegally performed, the courts tend to permit enforcement by an "innocent" party (i.e. one who has not performed illegally) but not by the guilty. On rare occasions, even the guilty party may be allowed to enforce the contract if his action can be asserted without reference to the illegality of the contract.

Fisher and Greenwood at 324.

83. For other examples of contracts to commit a crime or tort, see, e.g., 18 *Halsbury's* at paras. 115.210–115.211; *Chui and Roebuck* at paras 10.5.1–10.5.6; *Fisher and Greenwood* at 324–28.

84. *Chan Yau v Chan Calvin* [2014] 5 HKLRD 304, 323.

85. Id. at 325.

86. *Tang Teng Hong Tso v Cheung Tin Wah* [2014] 2 HKLRD 1032, 1038–39 [hereinafter *Tang Teng Hong Tso*].

87. *Chui and Roebuck* at para. 10.6: 'Contracts may be void because they are against public policy even though not illegal. The courts, while disapproving of them, do not regard them with the same severity as those which are strictly illegal.' The authors continue by noting: 'If merely one clause is void as against public policy, that clause may be severed, that is cut out, leaving the contract to stand without it . . . Collateral contracts will be valid as long as

they do not owe their existence only to the void part of the contract.' Id. at para. 10.6.2. For a more detailed discussion, see *Ho* at 480–512.

88. 18 *Halsbury's* at para. 115.213.
89. *Chitty* at para. 16-001.
90. Id. at para. 16-003.
91. Id. at para. 16-004.
92. Id. at para. 16-005.
93. *Best Sheen Development Ltd v Official Receiver* [2001] 1 HKLRD 866, 873.
94. Id. at 874 (citation omitted).
95. *Tang Teng Hong Tso* at 1039 (citation omitted).
96. *Ryder Industries Ltd v Chan Shui Woo* [2014] HKEC 1566, para. 22 (citation omitted).

Chapter 6

1. 18 *Halsbury's* at para. 115.290. It is beyond the purview of this book to examine in depth each of these grounds for discharging a contract. Only the most common grounds will be presented in general.
2. Id. at para. 115.291 states in part:

   > The basic rule is that a promisor must perform exactly what he undertook to do; and the question whether what has been done amounts to exact performance is a question in each case of the construction of the terms of the contract . . .
   >
   > In all cases, however, the requirement of exact performance is qualified by the *de minimis* rule, that is that minute and unimportant deviations from exact compliance will be ignored.

3. *Chitty* at para. 21-028. In similar, but more detailed, language is 18 *Halsbury's* at para. 115.292.
4. *Chitty* at para. 21-001. See *Ho* at 622–24.
5. *Chitty* at para. 21-033.
6. *Chui and Roebuck* at para. 6.2.1.
7. Id.
8. Id. at para. 6.2.2.
9. *Chitty* at para. 21-031. See *Ho* at 622.
10. *Variation of a contract* refers to changes or amendments made to an existing contract and is discussed below in section B. See, e.g., *Chitty* at paras. 3-076–3-080; 22-032–22-039.
11. 18 *Halsbury's* at para. 115.293.
12. *Chui and Roebuck* at para. 6.2.3.
13. See *Chitty* at para. 22-001; *Ho* at 637–41.

14. *Chui and Roebuck* at para. 6.3.
15. Id.
16. 18 *Halsbury's* at paras. 115.399; 115.403. The *BLIS Glossary* translates *assign a contract* as 轉讓合約.
17. *Chitty* at para. 19-077. See also *Chui and Roebuck* at para. 9.4.2.
18. 18 *Halsbury's* at para. 115.143.
19. Id. at para. 115.144.
20. Id. at para. 115.398. The *BLIS Glossary* translates *novation* as 約務更替.
21. 18 *Halsbury's* at para. 115.399. For a more detailed discussion, see id. at paras. 115.399–115.403.
22. 18 *Halsbury's* at para. 115.399.
23. Id.
24. *Chitty* at para. 22-025 notes the distinction between rescission and repudiation:

    > Where a contract is executory on both sides, that is to say, where neither party has performed the whole of his obligations under it, it may be rescinded by mutual agreement . . . A partially executed contract can be rescinded by agreement provided that there are obligations on both sides which remain unperformed. Similarly, a contract which has been fully performed by one party can be rescinded provided that the other party returns the performance which it has received and in turn is released from its own obligation to perform under the contract. The consideration for the discharge in each case is found in the abandonment by each party of its right to performance or its right to damages, as the case may be. A rescission of this nature must be distinguished from a repudiation by one party, which the other party may elect to treat as a discharge of the obligation, and from the right to rescind which is given to one party in cases of fraud, misrepresentation, duress and undue influence. . . .

    The *BLIS Glossary* translates *rescind the contract* as 撤銷合約, *rescission* as 撤銷, *repudiate the contract* as 悔約, and *repudiation of the contract* as 不履行……合約.
25. 18 *Halsbury's* at para.115.364.
26. *Chui and Roebuck* at paras. 6.5–6.5.1. See also 18 *Halsbury's* at paras. 115.364–115.372 for a more detailed analysis of the intricacies of repudiation. In particular, note the *proviso* of para. 115.365: 'Not every refusal to perform a part of the contract amounts to a repudiation which entitles the other party to treat the contract as at an end; there must be a refusal to perform something which goes to the root or essence of the contract.'
27. *Chui and Roebuck* at paras. 6.5–6.5.2.
28. *Fisher and Greenwood* at 226.

29. The *BLIS Glossary* translates *frustration of contracts* as 合約受挫失效. For a more detailed discussion of the subject, see *Butterworths* at 129–36.
30. *Davis Contractors Ltd v Fareham Urban District Council* [1956] AC 696, 729.
31. *Ocean Tramp Tankers Corp v V/O Sovfracht, The Eugenia* [1964] 2 QB 226, 238.
32. *National Carriers Ltd v Panalpina (Northern) Ltd* [1981] AC 675 (HL), 700.
33. *Chui and Roebuck* at para. 6.6.1.
34. 18 *Halsbury's* at para. 115.272.
35. Id. at para. 115.270 notes: 'The doctrine of frustration is in all cases subject to the important limitation that the frustrating circumstances must arise without fault of either party. The defence of frustration can therefore be defeated by proof of fault . . . Deliberate choice either not to perform or to put performance out of one's power will certainly be fault within this rule.'

    Chitty at para. 23-061 states: 'The essence of frustration is that it should not be due to the act or election of the party seeking to rely on it.' Thus, a contracting party cannot rely on 'self-induced frustration, that is, on frustration due to his own conduct or to the conduct of those for whom he is responsible'. Although the concept of self-induced frustration is clearly established as a matter of general principle, the precise limits of the doctrine have not been clearly established. It is merely a 'label' which has been used to describe: 'those situations where one party has been held by the Courts not to be entitled to treat himself as discharged from his contractual obligations'. Thus frustration has been held to be 'self-induced' where the alleged frustrating event was caused by a breach or anticipatory breach of contract by the party claiming that the contract has been frustrated (citations omitted).
36. In this regard, 18 *Halsbury's* at para. 115.274 notes: 'Whatever the alleged source of frustration, a contract is not discharged under the doctrine of subsequent impossibility and frustration merely because it turns out to be difficult to perform or onerous. Thus the parties will not generally be released from their bargain on account of rises or falls in price, depreciation of currency or unexpected obstacles to the execution of the contract, for these are ordinary risks of business. In particular, a party's insolvency or inability to get finance will not discharge him, unless, of course, the parties have agreed otherwise.'
37. The topic of breach and the remedies available therefore have already been introduced to the reader in the context of topics discussed elsewhere in this work, i.e., anticipatory breach, breach of condition, breach of warranty, fundamental breach, repudiation, and rescission. Discussion of these topics will not be repeated in this section.

Chapter 7

1. 18 *Halsbury's* at para. 115.378. The remedies mentioned in the latter portion of the quotation will not be presented in this work. However, they are mentioned so the reader is made aware that remedies other than those presented in this chapter might be available to an innocent party. For a more comprehensive

analysis of *damages*, see Harvey McGregor, *McGregor on Damages* (19th edition, 2014 and Supplement 1, 2015) [hereinafter *McGregor*].

2. *Chui and Roebuck* at para. 7.3.2: 'The usual purpose of an award of damages is to compensate the plaintiff for the loss caused by the breach. The object of damages is to put the injured party, so far as money can, into the same position as if the contract had been performed.' See generally *Ho* at Chapter 19 ('Remedies'). See also *Chitty* at para. 26-001; 44 *Halsbury's* at paras. 340.155–340.174.

3. *Richly Bright International Ltd v De Monsa Investments Ltd* [2015] HKEC 827 (CFA), paras. 15, 42 (citation omitted) [hereinafter *Richly Bright*].

4. But see *Attorney General v Blake* [2001] 1 AC 268, a court decision concerning the publication of the memoirs of a former British espionage agent contrary to the Official Secrets Act 1989. As damages, the Attorney General claimed the monies paid and to be paid to Blake by the publisher of his memoirs. This claim arose because Blake owed the government a duty not to profit from his former position as a Secret Intelligence Service member. There were two problems for the Attorney General to overcome. The first was that the Crown had suffered no loss as a result of the publication. The second obstacle was that English law at the time did not permit damages for breach of contract to be calculated by the financial benefits gained by the contract-breaker. The court overcame these problems by deciding that damages for breach of contract could be assessed by reference to the benefits gained by the wrongdoer rather than the loss suffered by the innocent party. The impact of the *Blake* case is analysed in 2003 *New LJ* 153.7079 (723); 2003 *Emp. Law & Lit.* 8.7 (33).

5. *Chitty* at para. 26-104: 'The term "remoteness of damage" refers to the legal test used to decide which types of loss caused by the breach of contract may be compensated by an award of damages.'

   The test is: 'A type or kind of loss is not too remote a consequence of a breach of contract if, at the time of contracting (and on the assumption that the parties actually foresaw the breach in question), it was within their reasonable contemplation as a not unlikely result of that breach.' Id. at para. 26-108.

   See also 44 *Halsbury's* at paras. 340.285–340.291. See *Richly Bright* at paras. 21–41 for further analysis of this topic.

6. *Chui and Roebuck* at para. 7.3.3: 'The defendant does not have to pay damages for loss which was not caused by the breach.'

   Chitty at para. 26-057: 'Although the issue of remoteness—whether a particular loss was within the reasonable contemplation of the parties—tends to the prominent one in cases of liability for damage in the law of contract, before any issue of remoteness can arise causation must first be proved: there must be a causal connection between the defendant's breach of contract and the claimant's loss. The claimant may recover damages for a loss only where the breach of contract was the "effective" or "dominant" cause of that loss.'

   See also *Butterworths* at 142–45; 44 *Halsbury's* at para. 340.288.

7. *Hadley v Baxendale* (1854) 9 Ex 341, 355.

8. *Chitty* at para. 26-077. See also *Butterworths* at 145–46.
9. *Mega Yield International Holdings v Fonfair Co Ltd* [2014] HKEC 1546 (CA), para. 28 (citations omitted).
10. For a more detailed discussion, see *Butterworths* at Part VII ('Remedies'); *Ho* at Chapter 19 ('Remedies').
11. For a more detailed discussion, see, e.g., 44 *Halsbury's* at paras. 340.246–340.248. See *McGregor* at paras. 4-002–4-036.
12. 44 *Halsbury's* at paras. 340.251–340.256. See also *McGregor* at paras. 4-036–4-048.
13. 44 *Halsbury's* at paras. 340.257–340.259. See also *Burrows* at 5–6, 25–29; *McGregor* at paras. 14-001–14-004, and 14-021–14-043.
14. 44 *Halsbury's* at paras. 340.249–340.250. See also *McGregor* at paras. 12-001–12-011.
15. *Chitty* at para. 26-042.
16. Id. at paras. 20-043–26-044.
17. See *Ho* at 746–60. The term *liquidated damages* is where the damages have been agreed and fixed by the parties. The term *unliquidated damages* is where the damages are to be assessed by a court. See *Chitty* at para. 26-007; 44 *Halsbury's* at paras. 340.240–340.242.
18. As noted by *Chitty* at para. 26-171: 'Where the parties to a contract agree that, in the event of a breach, the contract-breaker shall pay to the other a specified sum of money, the sum fixed may be classified by the courts either as a penalty (which is irrecoverable) or as liquidated damages (which are recoverable). The clause is enforceable if it does not exceed a genuine attempt to estimate in advance the loss which the claimant would be likely to suffer from a breach of the obligation in question.'
19. For a more detailed discussion, see, e.g., 44 *Halsbury's* at paras. 340.299–340.307.
20. *Dunlop Pneumatic Tyre Co v New Garage Co* [1915] AC 79, 86–88. See also *McGregor* at paras. 15-009–15-052.
21. *Elsley v J G Collins Insurance Agencies Ltd* (1978) 83 DLR (3d) 1, 15.
22. *Black's Law Dictionary* at 1297 defines *equitable remedy* as 'a nonmonetary remedy, such as an injunction or specific performance, obtained when monetary damages cannot adequately redress the injury'. See also *Butterworths* at 148–49.
23. As for the inadequacy of monetary compensation resulting in the remedy of specific performance, *Chitty* at para. 27-005 notes: 'The historical foundation of the equitable jurisdiction to order specific performance of a contract is that the claimant cannot obtain a sufficient remedy by the common law judgment for damages. Hence the traditional view was that specific performance would not be ordered where damages were an "adequate" remedy.'

24. 44 *Halsbury's* at para. 340.028 (p. 529).
25. See, e.g., id. at paras. 340.022, 340.028 (p. 530).
26. *Chui and Roebuck* at para. 7.4.1; *Chitty* at para. 27-034; 44 *Halsbury's* at para. 340.028 (pp. 527–28).
27. *Chui and Roebuck* at para. 7.4.1; 44 *Halsbury's* at para. 340.028 (p. 527). "Mutuality" means that specific performance will not be awarded *to* a party if it cannot be awarded *against* that party. *Fisher and Greenwood* at 141n34 (emphasis in original).
28. *Chitty* at para. 27-026. See also *Chui and Roebuck* at para. 7.4.1.
29. *Chitty* at para. 27-042.
30. *Chui and Roebuck* at para. 7.4.1; 44 *Halsbury's* at para. 340.022. See also *Chitty* at paras. 27-021–27-024.
31. *Chitty* at paras. 27-030–27-031. See also 44 *Halsbury's* at para. 340.022.
32. See, e.g., *Chui and Roebuck* at paras. 8.1–8.2.1. See also *Chitty* at paras. 26-182–26-192.
33. See, e.g., *Chui and Roebuck* at paras. 8.2.3–8.2.4; 44 *Halsbury's* at para. 340.305; *Chitty* at paras. 26-193–26-198.
34. See Chapter 4, section C.
35. See, e.g., *Chui and Roebuck* at paras. 8.11.1–8.11.2.
36. Id. at para. 8.11.1.

References

18 *Halsbury's Laws of Hong Kong* (LexisNexis Butterworths, 2nd edition, 2015 reissue)

35 *Halsbury's Laws of Hong Kong* (LexisNexis Butterworths, 2nd edition, 2013)

44 *Halsbury's Laws of Hong Kong* (LexisNexis Butterworths, 2nd edition, 2011)

Arjunan, Krishnan, and Abdul Majid bin Nabi Baksh, *Business Law in Hong Kong* (LexisNexis, 2nd edition, 2009)

Beale, H. G. et al., eds., 1 *Chitty on Contracts* (Sweet & Maxwell, 31st edition, 2012)

Black's Law Dictionary (West Group, 7th edition, 1999)

Burrows, Andrew, *A Restatement of The English Law of Unjust Enrichment* (Oxford University Press, 2012)

Butterworths Hong Kong Contract Law Handbook (LexisNexis Butterworths, 3rd edition, 2013)

Chan, Patrick, *Hong Kong English-Chinese Legal Dictionary* (LexisNexis Butterworths, 2005)

Chui, Carole, and Derek Roebuck, *Hong Kong Contracts* (Hong Kong University Press, 2nd edition, 1991)

Enonchong, Nelson, *Duress, Undue Influence and Unconscionable Dealing* (Sweet & Maxwell, 2nd edition, 2012)

Fisher, Michael J., and Desmond G. Greenwood, *Contract Law in Hong Kong* (Hong Kong University Press, 2nd edition, 2011)

Furmston, M. P. ed., *Cheshire, Fifoot & Furmston's Law of Contract* (Oxford University Press, 16th edition, 2012)

Ho, Betty M., and Stephen Hall, *Ho & Hall's Hong Kong Contract Law* (LexisNexis, 3rd edition, 2013)

Hong Kong Government Bilingual Laws Information System, *The English-Chinese Glossary of Legal Terms*

Lewison, Kim, *The Interpretation of Contracts* (Sweet & Maxwell, 5th edition, 2011)

McGregor, Harvey, *McGregor on Damages* (Sweet & Maxwell, 19th edition, 2014 and Supplement 1, 2015)

Stone, Richard, and James Devenney, *The Modern Law of Contract* (Routledge, 11th edition, 2015)

Suff, Marnah, *Essential Contract Law* (Cavendish Publishing, 2nd edition, 1997)

Wild, Charles, and Stuart Weinstein, *Smith & Keenan's English Law* (Longman, 16th edition, 2010)

Yeung, Clemence, *The Law of Unjust Enrichment in Hong Kong* (LexisNexis, 2008)

Index

www.ingramcontent.com/pod-product-compliance
Ingram Content Group UK Ltd.
Pitfield, Milton Keynes, MK11 3LW, UK
UKHW021833100926
8556IPUK00004B/317

9 789888 208432